WALKING THE WORLDS

Volume 1 | Number 2 | Summer 2015

BUILDING REGIONAL CULTUS

Walking the Worlds is a serious, peer-reviewed journal devoted to the exploration of spiritwork and polytheism from a broad spectrum of perspectives, traditions and disciplines. It is published twice a year on the solstices.

Managing Editor: Galina Krasskova
Editor-in-Chief: H. Jeremiah Lewis
Editorial Board: Edward Butler, Ph.D., P. Sufenas Virius Lupus, Ph.D.
Designer: Sarah Kate Istra Winter

Each issue of *Walking the Worlds* focuses on a different theme; please keep these in mind when submitting essays (poetry and fiction are not currently being accepted). The deadline for the Winter issue is October 1, and for the Summer issue it is May 1. Accepted submissions receive set monetary compensation, all rights reverting back to the author after six months. Essays should run approximately 2500-7000 words, excluding notes, and be accompanied by a brief biography and abstract. Illustrations and artwork may be accepted on a case-by-case basis. Please visit our website for full submission guidelines.

Upcoming Themes
Winter 2015: Magic and Religion
Summer 2016: Philosophy and Polytheism

Single issues are available for $20, and a full year subscription (two issues) for $30. Back issues are also available. Orders can be placed online. Appropriate advertisements may be accepted, with rates being $25 for a quarter-page, $45 for a half-page, and $75 for a full page. Specifications can be found on our website.

For more information, visit **WalkingTheWorlds.com**.

© 2015 Walking the Worlds
All rights reserved.

CONTENTS

From the Editor   1

Lares Alcobacenses: Naming the Gods of My Homeland   5
    HÉLIO PIRES

A Regional Conflict in Religiosity: Translating Worship Across Geographic Boundaries   12
    LYKEIA

Books Written on Soil: Developing an Irish-Based Practice of Inhabiting Sacred Landscapes   22
    P. SUFENAS VIRIUS LUPUS

A Typology of Spirits   34
    SARAH KATE ISTRA WINTER

Departed Countrymen: Grave Tending and the Chinese in California   39
    HEATHEN CHINESE

Adventures in Active Listening: Connecting to the Neighborhood   49
    VIRGINIA CARPER

The Lobsterman of Portland, Maine: Urban Cult Objects in a Heathen Context   58
    WAYLAND SKALLAGRIMSSON

Religions of Relation: Place, Hospitality, and Regional Cultus in Modern Polytheist Religion and Practice   62
    THEANOS THRAX

Ghost Stories of Gaul   86
    MORPHEUS RAVENNA

Olympos on the Banks of the Nile   95
    H. JEREMIAH LEWIS

Universality and Locality in Platonic Polytheism   106
    EDWARD P. BUTLER

Syncretism as Methodology of Localization: A Short Note on Antinoan Cultus in Antiquity and in the Syncretistic Present   119
    P. SUFENAS VIRIUS LUPUS

Sea, Earth, and What Came of It: Devotional Practice on the Information Ocean 125
   RAVEN KALDERA

Awakening the Land: Madness and the Return of Welsh Gods 131
   RHYD WILDERMUTH

From the Editor

In restoring our contemporary polytheisms, I can't think of any issue quite as important as regional *cultus*. This was one of the defining factors of ancient polytheisms and in many ways it continues to define our praxis, whether we actually realize it or not. What is regional cultus? Simply put, it refers to regional variants: within a tradition, and on a slightly smaller scale, within devotional and ritual practices for the individual Deities. There are, of course, many nuances to this, which the contributors for this issue discuss in detail.

We are at a crossroads as polytheists. We are hammering out an identity – for ourselves and our traditions – as distinct from the Pagan umbrella and as we do so, many important issues have come to light. One that I think deserves more attention than it receives is the fact that those of us practicing and developing our polytheisms in the United States, are in effect practicing Diaspora religions. In essence, we are practicing religions that developed in Europe, Asia, the Middle East, and Africa but doing so in the New World, outside of the cultural context that birthed them. That is significant. That has consequences for us as practitioners and for our approach as ritualists and devotees. We are isolated from the mindset of our ancestors by two thousand plus years of monotheistic conquest, but we are also isolated from the very lands and their attendant spirits in which our traditions first developed, land that holds the memory of many and much active cultus (the word is both singular and plural) on its soil.

There is, of course, a pro and a con to working within Diasporic traditions. We have the freedom to take our traditions in unexpected directions. There are cultural influences that we may choose to incorporate that never would have been possible on indigenous soil. The flip side of that is a deep-seated anxiety about legitimacy and authenticity that is, from my experience at least, largely lacking in those polytheists working on their native soil, amongst their own people. The experience of a practitioner of Romuva in Lithuania is dramatically different (for more reasons than simply the impact of resistance to Soviet occupation) from that of an American Heathen. Both are practicing indigenous polytheisms, but only one has the foundational support of doing so within one's tradition *and* on one's native soil. That we may be, for many generations native to the States only seems to add another layer of dis-ease to the process: the legacy of European immigrants in the US is one of colonialism, conquest, and genocide and though we ourselves may not be responsible for that, we reap, every day, the benefits of it. Contemporary American culture is also quite hostile to polytheism and its core values. All of this complicates this process, particularly when our own privilege prevents us from fully acknowledging our debts.

I've certainly seen this play out in Asatru and Heathenry. I wrote extensively about this in *Transgressing Faith: Race, Gender, and the Problem of "Ergi" in Modern American Heathenry* (Sanngetall Press, 2013). There seems to be an insecurity and anxiety around restoring traditions on foreign soil that has created some very reactionary, almost xenophobic threads within American Heathenry. It has led to a certain romanticization of the Heathen past, including the development of fundamentalist traditions like Theodism, which seek to reconstruct not just the religion, but the feudal social structure as well – regardless of the fact that such restorations bear little resemblance to actual historical structures. Most of all, there's a deep antagonism toward change and evolution within the tradition. I lay the responsibility for many of these trends, and the general fundamentalism of American Heathenry at the feet of this: we're in the Diaspora. There's an anxiety over not being on the religion's ancestral land. There's an anxiety over whether or not we're doing it right and with that, there's a certain fear of external influences. You see this in the aggressive insularity of American Heathenry, the outright hostility to anything outside the common norm.

Now, I'm focusing on Heathenry here, because it is the tradition that I practice. I think, however, there are vestiges of this in almost every American polytheism. Practices that would have been routinely accepted by our ancestors (oracles, divination, mysticism, possession, ecstatic rituals) terrify and antagonize contemporary polytheists because they are so incredibly outside of our dominant cultural norm. Even what it means that the Gods are real can cause moments of cognitive dissonance for contemporary practitioners. We are torn between two impulses: restoration and assimilation.

There are other factors that complicate this process of restoration as well: two thousand years of monotheistic indoctrination, the lack of intergenerational models for healthy practice of our traditions, the influence of the Protestant Reformation and modern and post-modern attitudes of disdain toward devotion, and the influence, in America, of uniquely fundamentalist strains of religion in general. We've an uphill battle to wage in restoring our traditions anew. Understanding that in addition to all of this, we are working within Diaspora traditions with all that may entail, might perhaps ease some of the communal anxieties and provide a better understanding of how to do this work of restoration well. After all, other religions have managed it. Lukumi and Candomble are both Diaspora traditions, birthed from the horrors of the slave trade and they are rich and flourishing across the world today.

So many issues to consider as we restore our traditions! It can easily seem overwhelming but one thing to always remember is that with our ancestors as with us today, there were the various permutations, sometimes quite colorful and exotic permutations of regional cultus. There never, ever was just **one** way to do any given polytheism. There were many, just as there were many ways to venerate each of the Deities, all dependent on region, on locale, on individual communities. That should give us tremendous freedom throughout this process. It also highlights the last of what some of us consider the sacred trine of polytheism: Gods, ancestors, and land. In a world in which the urban has come to largely replace the agricultural in our consciousness, it's all too easy to forget about that last point. Yet, it's all so crucial that we don't. This is in no way meant to marginalize the urban experience. I, for one, and quite happy living a non-agricultural lifestyle but I think it's easier to neglect veneration of the land spirits when we no longer directly depend upon their good graces for survival. Of course one can and should honor city spirits too – spirits of place are spirits of place, but there can be significant differences in approach.

I want to thank each and every one of our contributors for their explorations into what is a surprisingly complex topic. It is, however, one that has the grace of allowing us to work productively together, even when we may disagree. As we move forward in our restoration, let us do as our ancestors did: let us consider the complexities of regional cultus.

Galina Krasskova
Managing Editor

ERRATA

P. Sufenas Virius Lupus, "*Doíni, Dé 7 An-Dé*: Hero Cultus in Celtic Reconstructionist Polytheist Practice," *Walking the Worlds* 1.1 (Winter 2014), pp. 5-12.

On p. 11, the following short paragraph occurs in a list of entries related to possible Christian saints' days which can be adapted and adopted for honoring Irish heroes:

> **Medb** *(likewise not a goddess but instead a powerful queen): December 26th, which is the saint's day of Commán mac Fáelchon (whose patronymic means "son of Werewolf"!), patron of Co. Roscommon, where her capital of Cruachain (present day Rathcroghan) was located.*

    The author mistakenly gave the translation of "Fáelchon" as (the proper name) "Werewolf," rather than what it should be, which is more simply "Wolf." *Fáelchon* is the genitive of a compound word which is being used as a name here, which is *fáelchú*, composed of *fáel*, which literally means "howler" but essentially designates "wolf," and *cú* (which is lenited as it is the second element in a *dvandva*-style compound) is "dog," "wolf," or "unspecified canid." One finds that latter element most famously in the name of Cú Chulainn, which many translate as "the Hound of Culann," but which could just as easily be "the Wolf of Culann." Thus, the name in the case above means "howler-dog/howler-wolf," which is essentially just "wolf."

    The author mistook it for the word (which is attested as a name) of *Ferchú*, which is "man" *(fer)* plus "wolf/hound/unspecified canid" *(cú)*, not unlike *lycanthropos*, or even the word *werwolf* itself in Anglo-Saxon.

Lares Alcobacenses:
Naming the Gods of My Homeland

HÉLIO PIRES

> While local and regional cults are well documented in various polytheistic traditions, not every part of Europe has enough traces for an ancient cult to be revived. In some places, there is almost nothing to work with, forcing one to resort to direct contact, experiences of the place, a wider historical background and basic intuition. That is the case of my hometown, located in central coastal Portugal, and this article explains how I came to realize who its gods are and how I named them. In that process, an understanding of the ancient notion of god as a wide and not a narrow category, a realization of the overlaps between the Latin terms *deus*, *genius* and *lar*, as well as a knowledge of the various Roman-period inscriptions and altars found in western Iberia, were all essential elements that led me to an answer.

I was born in the small Portuguese city of Alcobaça, located in a valley just a few kilometers from the sea. I lived there until I turned 18, at which point I left for college. But more than the place where I spent the early years of my life, the city and its surrounding region are also my ancestral land: my paternal family has been in the area for at least three hundred years and my maternal forefathers are not without a link to it, too. So when, in 2013, I decided to add a local element to my Roman polytheistic practices, I had no doubt I would end up with something linked to my blood and bones. There was, however, one pivotal question to which there was no easy answer: who are the gods of my homeland?

Since I'm not a spirit worker, nor do I know any in the vicinity, direct contact and reply through trance work was not an option. At the start of my quest, I had only two tools: historical background and basic intuition. The former proved frustrating in its own way, for while there are traces of continuous human presence around Alcobaça since the Stone Age – including pre-Roman communities, Phoenicians, Romans and Visigoths – the information on individual gods is extremely scarce. There's only a Latin funerary inscription that mentions Minerva, a mosaic that presumably depicts Apollo, the drawing of what appears to be a human figure that was once carved in a now lost stone and the largely speculative idea, entertained by some (Espírito Santo 2005), that local Catholic religion has roots in older lunar cults, possibly of Phoenician origin or influence. While these traces are not without importance, none of them speaks of a clearly identifiable pre-Christian cult of a local or regional nature. And this is in stark contrast with the surrounding regions, where altars to Roman and pre-Roman deities have been found. Many of them mention well-know Iberian gods and goddesses, like Bandua, Trebaruna, Nabia and Ilurbeda, but also more obscure ones, like Aracus, Tabudico and Louciri, to which a link with Lugus has been suggested (Olivares Pedreño 2002: 64). I guess you could say that, when it comes to vestiges of pre-Christian religions, my homeland is a bit of a black hole. But despite that, historical background was not without its use, for while it was unable to produce a clear answer on the gods of Alcobaça, it nonetheless ended up supplying a model from which I was able to build something new.

One of the most important things I've come to realize as a result of my local quest is that there are gods everywhere. I know this sounds a bit like a no-brainer, yet there's more to it than most people believe. I don't mean it in a pantheistic sense of everything being a deity, but more in the animist perspective expressed by Thales of Miletus: everything is full of gods! The trees, the rocks, the rivers, the mountains, the beaches, the roads, the fields – they all have deities. If by now you're thinking that I'm actually talking about landwights or spirits, you're not entirely wrong, but neither are you entirely correct. See, after over one thousand years of Christian predominance, we've reached a point where we tend to think of religious matters in monotheistic terms. We use the word "faith" as a synonym of religion, even though that makes virtually no sense in a polytheistic context, and we've grown used to defining god as an entity that's high up and above everything else. All other beings in lower categories, even if they're still otherworldly or numinous, are something else. Christians speak of angels and saints, polytheists mention landwights and ancestors. But if you go back to a pre-Christian period, you find a very different notion of god. One that's not a privilege of an uppermost stratum, but a general quality of everything that's in some way numinous, no matter how small.

Historically, this is the case in Roman polytheism, which is where I'm coming from. The Latin word *deus* or god (feminine *dea*, plural *di*) was used for a vast range of beings, including some we would normally not qualify as deities: *Di Manes* (Divine Dead), *Di Parentes* (Divine Relatives), *Di Penates* (Household Gods), *Di Consentes* (the Greater Twelve or Olympian Gods), *Di Inferi* (Underworld Gods) and the *Di Indigetes*, which included minor entities like Cinxia, who watches over the bride's girdle. Robert Turcan calls them "good fairies" (2000: 18), but despite their lesser position in the divine hierarchy, the *Indigetes* were still called *di* or gods, as were the dead. Nymphs too were seen as goddesses, as evidenced by Latin inscriptions from Great Britain: in one, Brigantia is called *Dea Nympha* (*CIL* VII 875); in another, Coventina is addressed as *Nimpha Couentina* (*RIB* 1526). And what these examples show is that, at least in the ancient Roman world, the notion of god was similar to the

Japanese *kami* and unlike the Christian perspective we're used to: not as a narrow category applicable only to those on the highest stratum, but as a wide one that includes anything numinous, no matter its origin or scope. Hence the *Manes*, *Penates*, *Consentes* and *Inferi* are types of deities, subgroups of the larger god category.

They're not, however, clear-cut classes of divine beings and here lies another point that proved useful in my quest: the terminology is fluid and prone to overlap, sometimes extensively. This doesn't mean the various terms can be used freely or as synonyms, for while close, they nonetheless serve different practical purposes. For instance, because the *Manes* are the spirits of the dead, they're part of the underworld gods; but Persephone was never a living human being, so while She's also part of the *Inferi*, She's not one of the dead. A nymph is always a female deity, often associated with water, and one's ancestors have a place in one's home as Family Lares, though as *Manes* they're normally confined to graveyards. Simply put, different terms invoke different beings, but can also summon different aspects of the same entity. And that's because terminology is less about clear-cut categories, like species or types of creatures, and more about scope and function. A similar dynamics is true for the words *genius*, *deus* and *lar*, in that all three can cover a wide range of entities and hence overlap extensively, yet they're not synonyms. The most generic of them is *genius*, which can refer to any spirit, including that of a living being, whereas *deus* is applied only to non-humans or deceased humans. Also, both were and remain useful when addressing an unknown deity, either by calling it *genius* or using the expression *sive deus sive dea* (whether god or goddess). As for *lar*, it often has a link with landwights and a domestic, if not ancestral connotation. Thus the Family Lares were identified with one's ancestors, while the *Lares Viales* or gods of the pathways can be *genii loci*, the spirits of those entombed along the roads (which was a common practice in the ancient world), or both. The *Lares Compitales*, who presided over crossroads, are probably of a similar nature, though a more obscure case is that of the *Lares Permarini*, who watched over sailors. However, I have no difficulty seeing them as both seawights and spirits of those who lost their lives while sailing. The term *lar* could even be used for a greater god, as is the case of Silvanus, who's called *Lar Agrestis* or Rustic Lar in one occasion (*CIL* VI 646). He too is not without a domestic aspect (Dorcey 1992: 22-24) and, as a deity of the forest, He can only be expected to have a link with the landwights.

Roman-period traces from western Iberia show a similar pattern of fluidity and overlap: a group of gods named both as *Di* and *Lares Cairieses*, who may have been local deities, are known from the area of Castelo Branco, in Portugal; an inscription found in the Portuguese district of Chaves mentions the *Lares Tarmucenbaecis Ceceaecis*, perhaps identical to the *Dii Ceceaigis* who feature in another piece from further north, in the area of Ourense (Galicia, Spain); the ancient city of *Conimbriga*, a predecessor of the modern-day Coimbra, in

Portugal, produced a small altar to the *Genius Conimbricae*, as well as pieces to the *Lares Aquites*, who may have been aquatic gods or nymphs, and the *Lares Lubanci*, believed to have been tribal deities of a specific local clan; an altar dedicated to the *Lares Buricis* was found in the district of Braga (Portugal) and they may have been local gods, since the area where the piece comes from is known as Bouro; and another example is an altar found in Lugo (Galicia, Spain), which was dedicated to the *Lares Gallaeciarum* or the Galician Lares (Olivares Pedreño 2002: 54, 56-7, 74, 81-2 and 93).

This information eventually helped me clarifying the question of who are the gods of Alcobaça, but that didn't happen immediately. My first instinct was to go through the local historical record in search of direct answers, so when I failed to find them, I turned to intuition, which was the only tool I had left. And intuition told me I should go for a water goddess. Alcobaça is, after all, a water-rich area, full of rivers and streams, two of which join inside the city, and the nearby mountains house one of the country's largest underground reservoirs. Plus, there is the somewhat speculative idea that local Catholic cults have roots in older lunar cults, which are commonly related to the aquatic element, so it all seemed to fit. Of course, since I didn't know what to call the local goddess, I resorted to a well-known Iberian deity and added a local epithet, thus naming Her as *Nabia Alcobacensis*. At least that was the idea and it made sense, since Nabia is commonly associated with rivers and valleys. The etymology of Her name certainly points in that direction, given that it probably derives from **nau*, which is at the root of words like Latin *navis* (ship) and Spanish *nava* (valley) (Prósper 1997: 146). The several Iberian rivers and fountains named in a similar or identical fashion, like the Navia in Galicia, also reinforce that idea. And there's an historical precedent for local epithets, as in the case of an altar dedicated to *Nabia Sesmaca*, which was found in an area of Galicia that also produced an inscription that speaks of a castle or *castellum Sesm[...]* (Olivares Pedreño 2002: 234). Yet despite the fact that all of this made sense, offerings and prayers to *Nabia Alcobacensis* failed to produce any sign, omen or visible reaction of any sort. I wondered if I should pick a new name, if it simply needed to mature considering it was a new epithet or if I had to rethink the whole thing. In the end, I decided to let it rest. Sometimes, the more you look the less you find, so I gave time a chance to slowly produce an answer.

It was not until January of 2015 that things started falling into place. My first epiphany was when I joined a trekking group for a morning walk into the local woods. As I found myself on a narrow path, surrounded by oak and pine trees and walking along streams that slithered through rocks and roots, I thought of a god I had thus far failed to consider: Silvanus! I was so focused on the aquatic element that I missed the green around it and the many ways through which the Roman god of trees and forests can be connected to Alcobaça: a document from the middle of the twelfth century describes the region as a *silva* (Nascimento 2007: 74), which is what is was for a long time and still is in many parts; the southern end of one of the country's largest pine forests is just a few kilometers away and Silvanus is not without a close link with the nymphs, not in the lustful manner of Pan or Faunus, but in a more fatherly way, it seems (Dorcey 1992: 43-5); the god is also associated with cattle, even being called *sanctissimus pastor* or most holy shepherd in one instance (Dorcey 1992: 21) and He is commonly depicted with a pruning knife, in some cases even with a batch of fruit, which resonates well with the rural traditions of Alcobaça and the economic importance of the local fruit production. Of course, there was also a lot of potential concerning the goddess Nabia, so I took a more careful approach with Silvanus. One morning, I went up a wooded slope, poured some offerings in front of a pine tree and asked Him if He was the god of hometown or, at the very least, if He was willing to be. The night after, I had a dream where something crossed the Pyrenees and moved in from the east. Whether it was a reference to how Latin gods were brought by the Romans and went native, a more recent move by someone or just my mind playing tricks, I know not. But several days later, something else dawn on me.

When I first started working on this matter back in 2013, my intention was to find *a* local god or goddess. Not landwights or the dead, which people don't normally see as actual gods, but one entity along the lines of Jupiter, Minerva, Apollo or Ceres. In other words, a "proper" deity, because I was working on the assumption that a god has to be an entity that's on the highest place of the hierarchy. But as I mentioned before, that is a misguided notion that owes more to monotheism than ancient Roman polytheism. The *di* weren't just the greater gods of Olympus, they were also the powers of the underworld, the *indigetes*, the nymphs, the landwights, the housewights, the dead. The mighty ones of above and below, but also the smaller ones of individual trees, rocks, rivers and trails, as well as the dearly departed. There are gods everywhere, not because everything is a deity, but because the *genii loci* and spirits of the deceased are gods too – rightly, properly and without scare quotes. And when I realized this, I found the answer I was looking for.

I know who the gods of my homeland are! They are the *genii* and nymphs of its trees, hills and mountains, its streams and springs, its roads and beaches, its orchards, fertile fields and hard rocks. They are the spirits of the dead, both human and animal, claimed and forgotten, native or mere travelers who passed away on the local roads and remained tied to them. Perhaps the kings, queens and princes entombed in the local monastery are part of the host, while others are the unclaimed dead who wander through the land. And also among the *Lares Alcobacenses* are my own ancestors, who lived and died in this land, whose animals lived and died here. They too are *genii loci* and when their bodies melted into the ground, they became a part of the local soil, so the landwights know me because the land has blood and bones of my family, my blood and bones. These are the gods of my homeland! Countless, diverse and tied to the place I was born in and hopefully will one day be buried in.

After realizing this, I wondered what to call them, collectively. I can name some individually, but the vast majority remain anonymous to me, so a comprehensive name was needed. It could have been *Di*, it could have been *Genii*, which would not be outside Roman tradition, but since they're the gods of my ancestral land, a term with an ancestral connection seemed to be the most appropriate. I therefore picked *lar*, a choice reinforced by the aforementioned historical examples from western Iberia, like the *Lares Buricis*. So I started addressing the gods of my homeland as *Lares Alcobacenses*. And it felt real, it felt close, almost palpable.

Now, this doesn't mean the idea of local epithets for Nabia and Silvanus has become pointless. As mentioned, both resonate with the regional countryside, so the potential for a connection is still there. Plus, in the process, I ended up including the two of them in my religious practices, so now each have a yearly feast in my calendar. And as a result of worshipping two gods that have much in common with my homeland, I may yet add them to the *Lares Alcobacenses*. Not as *the* local gods, but as named or even leading figures of the local host. One possibility that I'm considering is Silvanus as *Lar Alcobacensis* and hence first or leader among the *Lares Alcobacenses*. Given His connection to nymphs, it would not be outside historical precedent. And there's also a practical reason to it, in that I'm not always in my hometown, so if I want to address and honor its gods, physical distance may be a problem. The spirits of the dead may be reachable, but the same may not be said of the *genii* of individual streams, rocks, hills and trees. To those, *in situ* worship is probably required, yet when that's not possible, the notion of a divine intermediary can be useful. In other words, having a localized aspect of a supralocal god that can act as a link with strictly local deities. Silvanus, as *Lar Alcobacensis*, could fill in that role.

This would also solve the question of when to honor the Lares of my homeland on a monthly basis. The Calends, Nones and Ides, which translate as the first, the fifth or seventh and the thirteenth or fifteenth days of each month, respectively, are a possibility, since that's when I worship my ancestors and housewights. But if I associate Silvanus with the *Lares Alcobacenses*, then the answer could be the twenty-third. The reason for that is that November 23 is the national Day of the Native Forest in both Portugal and Spain. While most of the world celebrates Arbor Day around the start of spring, the southern European climate makes late autumn the best time of year to plant trees, and since Silvanus is their god, the Day of the Native Forest seems like the perfect date to honor Him. Thus, following the principle of marking monthly what is celebrated annually, the twenty-third of each month would be the day to pay tribute to Silvanus and the gods of my homeland, wherever I may be.

Another possibility that I'm considering is pairing up Silvanus and Nabia, in the manner of Sucellus, with whom Silvanus was historically identified, and Nantosuelta, who resembles Nabia somewhat (Olivares Pedreño 2002: 222-7). It would be a combination of the Lady of springs and rivers that flow from the nearby mountains with the Lord of woodland and fields in the valleys, where the local gods dwell and wander. Almost like king and queen of the *Lares Alcobacenses*. Or, should the goddess remain silent about it, I may go for a more generic Silvanus and the *Nymphae Alcobacenses*, thereby highlighting a group of the Lares in a manner that leaves a local Nabia or Diana implied.

There are obviously several elements I still need to figure out, so during the next several months, if not years, I'll be doing more research, meditation and, to the best of my limited ability, divination on where the Gods stand. But whatever the case, whomever, if anyone, takes on a leading and representative role, I now know who the deities of my homeland are. They are the *Lares Alcobacenses*, the gods of the place, and they're all around.

Works Cited

Dorcey, Peter F. 1992. *The cult of Silvanus: a study in Roman folk religion*. Columbia studies in the classical tradition 20, Leiden: Brill.

Espírito Santo, Moisés. 2005. *Cinco Mil Anos de Cultura a Oeste*. Lisboa: Assírio e Alvim.

Nascimento, Aires A. ed. 2007. *A Conquista de Lisboa aos Mouros: relato de um cruzado*. 2nd edition, Lisboa: Veja.

Olivares Pedreño, Juan Carlos. 2002. *Los Dioses de la Hispania Céltica*. Madrid: Real Academia de la Historia, Universidad de Alicante.

Prósper, Blanca. 1997. "El nombre de la diosa lusitana Nabia y el problema del betacismo en la lenguas indígenas del Occidente Peninsular", in *Ilu. Revista de Ciencias de las Religiones*, n. 2, Madrid: Universidad Complutense de Madrid, pages 141-149.

Turcan, Robert. 2000. *The Gods of Ancient Rome*. Translated by Antonia Nevill, New York: Routledge.

Hélio Pires is a 35 year old Roman polytheist from Portugal. His domestic pantheon includes gods from different cultures, but his practice remains overwhelmingly Roman. He's also a devotee of Mercury, medieval Historian, blogger, amateur sporter, environmentalist and dog-friend.

A Regional Conflict in Religiosity: Translating Worship Across Geographic Boundaries

LYKEIA

> Lykeia explores some of the problems and resolutions to worshipping deities from vastly different climates from one's own native home. She provides solutions to common problems encountered and follows with discussion regarding how her own worship of the Mediterranean god Apollon has over time become adapted to life in a subarctic environment.

There is a unique challenge for worshipers when they are establishing a local cultus to gods whose myth and worship originates in vastly different geography. Such challenges are present not only in local wildlife which can vastly impact the symbolic, iconic and heraldic presence of the god, but also in weather patterns and climate due to extreme regional separation. This can impact not only the relationship you establish with the gods, but also how that relationship is expressed. This is due in part because the gods, as conceived in their native cultures, are tied to their native landscapes in complex ways. That is to say, that which is sacred to a given god or goddess of a particular culture is tied not only to the topography of the area, but also to what vegetation may be present, the food available for consumption, and animals that share their environment. This vastly influences the way people have communicated with and given worship to their gods. Inviting a god to a vastly different geography, topography and climate presents many obstacles. This foremost requires acknowledging that even with one's best efforts one's regional cultus will not appear identical to the native one.

Modifications of a non-native worship in your household will often include local substitutions. This is not to say that you will not get lucky and find some common heraldic animals and vegetation that can also be found in your local region; however, the relationship that these things have with your region may not be in the same vein as in your god's native region. This would especially be the case for aggressively invasive plants and released wildlife, as is the case with wild boars in the Americas and Australia, and snakes in Hawaii that often have a negative impact on the region. That said, many native plants and animals have large geographic habitation ranges. Animals such as various kinds of native cattle, wolves, various birds such as eagles and hawks, wild pigs or boars, and rodents are pretty common in numerous regions in familiar forms. Then there are the farm animals that have become regional creatures due to their importation with colonization and human migration. However, just as often there are no exact matches for a particular sacred plant or heraldic animal of the god or goddess with whom one is establishing a religious relationship. There is certainly precedent for regional substitutions for preferred animals for various activities, such as the preference of mules over oxen as laboring beasts in some parts of Hellas. This would doubtless impact the regional relationship with any deity connected to the laboring activity, such as the unique sacredness of mules to Vesta in Rome for their use in her mills for grinding grain, or the oxen to Demeter in their use for tilling the fields for sowing. This is important because heraldic animals are associated with gods not only as symbols of the nature of the god, such as bulls and lions associated with gods of kingly or queenly authority and attributes, but also because they are an important part of the activity of the god in question. Horses, for instance, are typically sacred in many places to charioteer deities such as Hera, Apollon, and Helios, and oxen for gods associated with agricultural activity, not only the more obvious deities such as Demeter, but also those, such as Selene, who have influence on plant growth and cultivation.[1]

As such, when the variance of one's regional locality calls for a substitution, the first thing that is important for consideration is whether the animal associated with the deity one is giving worship to is heraldic because of functional characteristics, for symbolic characteristics, or both. This will have a heavy weight in how one determines an appropriate substitution. A bull or ox, for instance, will commonly have both symbolic and functional associations with many gods, as many "king gods" also have some functioning role in agricultural activity, while a serpent is almost always heraldic for symbolic reasons as a representation of the hidden, chthonic or ambiguous nature of a deity. In some ways, functional heraldic animals are almost easier to substitute, as in the case above where there was a regional preference for mules over oxen for their agricultural use as work animals. In the case of a charioteer deity who is being honored in a climate inhospitable to horses it is appropriate to consider regional beasts used for transportation vehicles such as reindeer, sled dogs, oxen, mules etc.

In this case one needs to distinguish between a charioteer god whose functional activity is part of their domain and a god who simply has a chariot that he or she uses, which may be pulled by any number of myriad beasts that are chosen for symbolic purposes. In the latter case one is not substituting a function creature but is in the realm of symbolic heraldic beasts. An example would be the dove-drawn chariot of Aphrodite. The doves here are not associated with the charioteer function, but rather serve her in pulling her

---

[1] Gladstone, William Ewart. *Homer* (New York: D. Appleton and Company, 1881): 137.

chariot because of their symbolic relationship with the goddess. It could be a visual-poetic way of demonstrating that the goddess comes on the wings of love. Naturally doves, and their close relatives the pigeons, are pretty abundant everywhere in a large variety of environments and landscapes making a substitution unnecessary in most cases. However, the hind-drawn chariot of Artemis presents a different matter, as deer are not universally common, and their relatives are not always appropriate substitutes. This would be a case of basing the substitution on the symbolic nature of the hind and its association with the goddess. With a hind we are looking at a swift beast of prey, typically horned, and relating to a concept of divine elevation or spiritual height, rendering said deity quite unapproachable or untouchable, but also desirable as something which is hunted out. Whether or not the animal is literally used to pull any kind of vehicle is irrelevant in this case, so when making a regional substitution it will be largely these qualities above that one will be looking at. The presence of antelope rather than deer decorating the form of Artemis in Ephesus suggest that locals identified the beast with the goddess as an appropriate substitution for the climate of Asia Minor. However when we come into more northern regions, substitutions may not be of such a visual similarity. Being merely of the same general family as deer is not enough to qualify an animal as a regional substitution. For instance, a moose does not make a great substitution for a deer. While not particularly slow, they don't tend to possess the kind of speed and agility associated with deer. However, among the Thrakians, Melians, Boeotians and generally most of Hellas in the early end of the Classical era the association of hares with Artemis may serve the same purpose as the association with hinds. Xenophon brings some clarity to the matter in attributing the creation of game and hounds to Apollon and Artemis, combined with known images of the hare provided in a devotional context for both gods as hunters. He also states that live newborn hares were often given as gifts to the goddess. Although not horned, long-eared hares make a good substitution in this case as creatures not only for their historical symbolic associations but also for their abundant presence through many regions and geographies; likewise lynx in more northern climates, whose spotted fur not only carries marking not unlike that of the spotted hind skin but like the hare is prized for its warmth and would have been actively hunted.[2]

While heraldic animals are important features of the cult in how the god is portrayed and may be viewed as symbolic vessels and representatives of a deity, perhaps the most important substitutions that may vary from region to region would be those things which would be important offerings outside of the iconographic. Plant life and substances derived from local vegetation are an

---

[2] Schaus, Gerald P. *Stymphalos: The Acropolis Sanctuary, Volume 1* (University of Toronto Press, 2014): 40.

important feature of what we give to our gods on a regular basis. While most people are spoiled in the modern market for access to items that we would not be able to otherwise have in native climates, it is important to remember that this removes one even further from the nature of what one is giving to the gods. Wine, even if people are not wine makers, has a lot more meaning to people from regions with vineyards than in regions where the climate is inhospitable to grape cultivation. For instance, this vine is an important part of the cultures of the Mediterranean, whereas this is not the case in other climates where the grape is not sustainable, even in its hardier hybrid form, for production of wine and the maintenance of vineyards outside of possibly minimal personal use. For individuals who live in the subarctic or in tropical zones this can mean that the worshiper may have less spiritual relationship and identification with wine than those who live in environments more similar to the Mediterranean climate, and such offerings may be imbued with less meaning on a personal level. This does not invalidate traditional offerings, but rather it should open worshipers up to alternatives to use in more regular offerings that have a relationship to their native regions and save the imports for special occasions.

For wine, the most important value seems to be the fermentation process, the organic transformation of liquid substance into alcohol. It is the production of the divine substance from the destruction of the original material, quite appropriate for a sacrificial god such as Dionysos. The sacredness is in the transforming nature of the wine, and its substance is imbued with these qualities. The same would hold true for mead, which was also known in Hellas and was likely the sacred substance that Aristaios, the son of Apollon and the Thessalian princess Kyrene, offered in competition with the wine of Dionysos.[3] Although the gods opted for the wine of Dionysos as the most sacred of substances, the value of mead should be noted as an ideal substitution for its worth as measured against wine. As fermentation (which occurs in nature even without human assistance) appears to be the most important feature, forms of distilled alcohol (which requires human intervention after the initial fermentation) would be a poor substitute. There can be an argument made for the alteration of the conscious mind through imbibing alcohol that would make distilled spirits valid through the functional nature of wine. However, it is dubious that this is the most important characteristic of the sacredness of wine. Therefore, when choosing substitutes it would probably be of greater value to go with fermented substitutes over distilled substitutes that rely entirely on human processing. As many regions in the north have strong cultural attachments to beer or mead it can inspire possible substitutes that can be used

---

[3] Cook, Arthur Bernard, "The Bee in Greek Mythology," *The Journal of Hellenic Studies* 15 (1895).

depending on what is common in your region. Generally speaking, breweries can be found in most places in some form or another, or if you are adventurous enough to make your own home brew of some variety of wine, mead or beer from local fruits, this can be a powerful substitute. One should keep in mind that some areas do have local wineries that, while grapes are not grown in the region, do use infusions of local fruits into the wine base to create something regionally unique.

With a bit of time invested, one will also become familiar with what crops are grown locally, and what kind of flora is native to one's region. Books from the local library can be used to familiarize oneself with local plants, and visits to the local Farmer's Market are highly encouraged to get an idea of what crops are local and in season. Over time one will come to recognize certain appropriate regional plants that make effective substitutes for offerings and ritualistic purposes. This comes down to paying attention to one's environment and immersing oneself in it in addition to possibly studying local native lore regarding the plants. Understand what non-native plants have taken root and are thriving while keeping in mind that the invasiveness of some species in their non-native homes may impact the original character of the plant as understood from its native environment. Through this process one will likely also discover certain sacred haunts of one's gods that may become important spiritual fixtures in one's life, whether this be a stream through a heavily wooded area, a particularly rugged peak, or a certain cove. Becoming aware of one's environment not only improves one's ability to find substitutes, but also to recognize the presence of the gods in one's region, and to understand how the region impacts how one's god manifests to one as they take on regional characteristics.

The remainder of this article will address the above in regard to Apollon in the subarctic region of Alaska. Given the extreme difference between the subarctic and Mediterranean regions, it serves as an example of the challenges that one encounters in transplanting the gods to very different environments. In this case more familiar forms become downplayed, whereas more ambiguous and less prominent forms of the god are more expressed.

Unlike the Mediterranean, in which Apollon's half of the year, from spring to autumn, expresses specific cultivation cycles, in the subarctic there is very little cultivation going on throughout most of his season. In the former case planting is done in the winter with new crops sprouting well before the beginning of spring during the wintry rainy season, whereas in the latter case plant life doesn't begin to sprout until April or May. The problem here is that during Thargelia when people celebrated the green ear of wheat in May, in far northern latitudes crops do not have any such growth at this time. Apollon's season, which deals with the maturation of plants for harvest, becomes a hurried season in which plants must go from seed to full maturity within the span of just three or four months. Crops that can rapidly grow with long hours of sunlight do well, but other crops that need longer growing seasons fail. It is only in certain pockets that grain crops can be grown at all, such as around the valley area of Palmer which features Alaska's only dairy and the majority of its farmable land. For many Alaskans in more northern regions, regional relationship to grains at all would be all but absent. Apollon's important relationship with the grain cycle in Attica and throughout Ionia becomes considerably less important in Alaska, whereas his herding characteristics recognized by Homer and throughout many regions of Hellas become more pronounced in Alaska, with reindeer herding providing the local specialty of meat. Apollon as a hunting god, far less known despite Xenophon's account of Artemis and Apollon as the gods who invented game and hounds, also becomes far more prominent as most of this region is dependent on subsistence hunting and tourism associated with wild game and hunting.

Given the balance between herding and hunting activities, and how interconnected they are, it is not surprising then that Apollon Lykeios and Apollon Karneios would be highly important forms of Apollon as manifesting in this region. He is the wolfish god, overseer of herds and hunter of prey, god of the chlamys[4] and herding staff. He is Agraios. He is also the bringer of the fruits and ripening god, as is also applicable to Karneios. There is very little of the more fixed Delphic temple god here, but rather a roaming god, migratory with the herds and flocks, draped in a wolf pelt for his cloak amid rugged landscapes, along the summits of the mountains from which the glaciers hang, beside the marshes, through the tundra and forests, perhaps at times driving a sleigh or small chariot. The places where the migrant beasts dwell are where he is found, as he herds them to their summer breeding grounds, the swans nesting in the brush of the tundra where the caribou drop their calves, and the moose coming down from the mountains into the valleys to bear their young. The mountains are most especially his, by which he provides the perfect conditions in the valley for the growth of crops. Even as Apollon was anciently recognized as a god who brought forth the ripening of the crops, and as Karneios holds the pinecone that indicates he holds back the rains to make maturation of the vines possible, in such an extreme environment he is necessarily the god who provides the conditions for such ripening to occur for both the native and non-native crops.

In the subarctic the way the seasons are measured is also quite different. In the far northern latitudes, given that the seasons cannot be practically divided along agricultural lines as they are in most places, the seasons are light-based, the winter half of the year following the autumn equinox in which the year falls into extreme darkness, and the summer half of the year in which the region develops extremely long periods of light. This does not mean that Apollon here

---

[4] Smith, William. *Dictionary of Greek and Roman Antiquities* ("Chlamys"), 273.

should be confused with Helios, in fact in the Alaskan region the light bringer, Raven, is quite distinct from the sun. In association with the raven or crow in Apollon's own traditional worship, this reinforces the differentiation between Apollon and Helios while reaffirming their close relationship, as in variations of Alaskan myths the Raven is responsible for liberating the sun from the house of the creator to illuminate all of the world. This is on par with Lykeios, who is as much a god of light in the generic sense as he is the wolfish god. While the Trickster persona is an odd fit for Apollon, the often-benevolent function of Raven toward humanity fits well with the character of Apollon. Certainly the cunning and ambush that is required in hunting speaks to something more cunning and calculated in Apollon's nature that is typically ignored, even though it is a trait recognized in predators such as wolves with which he is identified. In these cases Raven can be seen as a spirit that is a powerful ally of Apollon, or as a part of the influence of his domain. The strong presence of ravens in winter, however, is at odds with the concept of Apollon's winter departure. In fact, despite the shortened days of winter, the strong presence of wolves and ravens in the winter months are more affirming of Apollon's continued presence as a torch-bearing god through the darkest nights of winter as he races before the packs and issues forth the flocks of ravens. Given that the far northern latitudes are highly subsistence-based, the provision of foodstuff is a yearlong endeavor that would be undertaken by Apollon and Artemis throughout the year in different forms as necessary. This is strikingly different from ancient Hellas, where game hunting became more of a seasonal leisure activity of the few due to the scarcity of wild big game.

Getting to know the relevant forms of Apollon as he manifests regionally is an important part of honoring him in each locality where he is worshiped. Although Lykeios and Karneios are the among the strongest manifestations of Apollon in the far northern latitude, there are many other specific features in this region which Apollon can be found tied to in additional household and civic functions the god expresses everywhere. Apollon Thermios, the god of the hot springs, is regionally relevant in the northern latitudes wherever one can often find hot springs. Apollon Aktaios is present at every harbor, which in Alaska are particularly important not only for the goods, food and materials imported from the southern states, but for the tourism the state is economically dependent on. Apollon Nymphegetes is also quite apparent, since the wild spaces are so important for subsistence and nature-dependent tourism. The nymphs of the mountains, marshes, rivers, springs and seas are his companions here as much as they were in Hellas. Apollon preserves and oversees the natural spaces in cooperation with his twin and the nymphs of the various landscapes, which can be lumped under the providence too of Apollon Nomios, protector of pastures.

It is important to stress that the forms in which Apollon manifests vary from region to region as they did in the city-states of Hellas. More agrarian parts of the Midwest or in the "Bread Basket" of the country may see less if any of the above epithets and more of Apollon Smintheus and Apollon Parnopios as protector of crops from mice and locusts, or in ranching lands Apollon Lykeios may come to the fore as protector of cattle from wolves and coyotes. It is also natural that regionally specific names may come to the fore. At the highest peak of the Alaska Range that provides a barrier to the northern arctic, Apollon Denalios, lord upon Mt Denali, has been asserted. Denali, a name that means "The High One" in the language of the Koyukon people, not only has a long history of being a place of wolves, while the peaks were abundant with mountain goat and wild sheep, but was also considered by the local natives the home of the sun upon its icy peak.[5]

There are few traditional sacred flora and fauna that are native to the region, wolves and ravens aside. Pines are plentiful, foretelling the coming of winter as their cones open up to release their seeds. Yet the sacred laurel cannot survive transplanted, and frankincense is not indigenous, not that it is in most regions. In fact, polytheists finding local alternatives for their worship could help the problematic excessive use of frankincense. The purifying fumigating nature of frankincense can be locally supplemented with plants of similar properties. In Alaska this can be especially found in cedar chips or beads of pine resin, whereas the holy laurel could be supplemented with non-native rowans that particularly thrive in the region as powerful wards against evil and in association with boundaries (both seasonal and domestic), and as an important purification plant as the laurel was implemented over thresholds and in ritualistic use, or in the domestic application of kitchen-grown rosemary sprigs. Sadly nearly every flowering plant sacred to him, such as crocus and hyacinth, while it will grow if planted in gardens, is not hardy in this zone and would have to replanted yearly. Nor does the crocus grow in the seasonally appropriate time for when it was offered, which was in winter in Hellas. Violets, irises and peonies however are abundantly planted and a worshiper would be wise to take advantage of the summer month to grow them. They do very well in this climate, and make an appropriate all-around offering to Apollon. Jane Harrison makes a connection between the peony and his title Paian, and Pausanias refers

---

[5] Mech, L. David. *The Wolves of Denali* (University of Minnesota Press, 2003): 22; Bernabaum, Edward. *The Spiritual and Cultural Significance of National Parks*, IIP Digital, 2008. Web Accessed 03/25/15 <http://iipdigital.usembassy.gov/st/english/publication/2008/06/20080630161601cmretrop0.3615381.html#axzz3VRP8FI8B>;
Berntsen. *Mount McKinley Monument: Surveyors Scale Slopes of Summit: Benchmark Set on Mighty Mount McKinley* (originally pub. Berntsen SurveyLog Vol 1, No.1, 1990). Web Accessed 03/25/15 <http://www.berntsen.com/Famous-Monuments/Mount-McKinley- Monument>.

to Iamos, a son of Apollon possessing hair the color of the violets, or irises in other translations, where he was nursed on honey by serpents. The purple wild aconite, or wolf's bane, is also an appropriate offering to Lykeios who keeps the packs in check. Larkspur, which closely resembles aconite, is also a plant that grows wild throughout much of the subarctic and is theorized by some to have been the original Hyakinth. Additionally, while Alaska typically lacks many of his sacred trees such as poplars, ashes and cypresses, crab apples and hybrid apples can be offered to Apollon Maleates, "Apollon of the apple."[6]

For sacred beasts that can be part of one's devotional worship through offerings and in iconography, griffins as mythological creatures still work and in fact as creatures said to live in northern mountains they might have an even greater significance to those dwelling at more northern latitudes as protectors of Apollon's abode, as well as a tie to the natural gold stores within the streams and hills of Alaska. In addition to the aforementioned hares, ravens and wolves, swans are also in keeping with tradition. Trumpeter swans, the largest variety of swan known for their resonating French horn-like vocalizations, migrate from all over the U.S. to Alaska around the beginning of April to their nesting grounds. As such, their return signifies the height of Apollon's season and the return of the growing period as they are among the earliest migratory birds following the white geese. Red-tail hawks, merlin and peregrine falcons keep with Apollon's associations with raptors for their speed and dominance of the heavens, second only to the bald eagles. That is about where it ends. Although goats are kept by many local farmers, as evident at the yearly fair, goats do not have enough of a significant presence in the state other than the wild mountain goats that are hunted along the high cliff areas to warrant an exclusive representation of the herding god. When it comes to herd beasts, reindeer would be more appropriate perhaps to substitute for offerings when honoring Apollon Agraios and Apollon Karneios, or to supplement goat-types of offerings. Meanwhile, the black-tail deer live only in the most southeasterly parts of the state and so in most places in Alaska likely would not be a significant part of his regional worship. Whereas there are wolf spiders, mice and shrew closer to the Gulf of Alaska around Anchorage and throughout the southeast, other important cult animals such as lions, locusts, boars and snakes (or any reptiles) have zero presence in the region, nor are there any appropriate regional substitutes. They get relegated strictly to symbolic association with the

---

[6] Raudvere, Catharina and Jens Peter Schødt. *More than Mythology: Narratives, Ritual Practices and Regional Distribution in Pre-Christian Scandinavian Religions* (Nordic Academic Press, 2012): 212-13; Harrison, Jane. *Myths of Greece and Rome* (1928): 33-39; Theoi.Com *Flora I: Plants of Greek Myth* (2010-11) Web Accessed 03/25/15 <http://www.theoi.com/Flora1.html> Callimachus, "To Apollon": 132 v. 79-94; Pausanias :6.2.3

god, without regional connection. In other words, a half step below griffins, that at least have a regional symbolic relationship.

Despite the shift in focus and the difference in how Apollon tends to manifest in this latitude, which may seem to have less in common with how the god is expressed popularly, adapting one's cult to adjust to regional differences makes the god more "present." Or rather, it makes one more aware of the god's presence, instead of focusing strictly on more abstract understandings of the god without any real world connection of them to where one lives. That is to say, that one can identify the presence and power of one's god in the local environment where one lives, rather than relying on how one imagines the god expressing himself in another environment with which one is not familiar. This does not remove features of the cult that can be appreciated symbolically. Serpents are still an important part of Apollon's cult regardless of where one lives, even if they play a more abstract symbolic role rather than an intimate personal role, where the Wolf Spider in Alaska would have more local "presence" than the cognitive symbol of snake. These differences are to be appreciated as they are what make his regional cult (and likewise for other gods) unique from place to place, and yet at the same time containing a continuity with his traditional worship.

> Lykeia is a devotee and servant of Apollon, and Artemis, living in the subarctic of Alaska with her two daughters and significant other. As both an Orphic Hellenic and a follower of Sanatana Dharma, much of her life, writing and work is colored by these spiritual philosophies and way of living. Much of her free time is committed to devotional art (in form of sculptures and paintings) and religious writings which comprises the sole use her BA in History. When not engaged in these things, gardening, music and dance are her passions. You can follow her blog at lykeiaofapollon.wordpress.com and view her devotional art on her deviantart account at templeofapollon.deviantart.com.

Books Written on Soil: Developing an Irish-Based Practice of Inhabiting Sacred Landscapes

P. SUFENAS VIRIUS LUPUS

Toponymic lore in Ireland, in the form of place-name etiologies which often have folk etymologies based in word-play, has its own genre, known as *dindshenchas*, "lore of famous places," which is also found throughout other genres and major works of medieval Irish literature. These stories of how significant locations got their names reflect a "genealogy of landscape" (A. Joseph McMullen), and model what modern polytheists who practice Irish-derived traditions should strive for in relation to their own local places of significance and their relationships to the deities, spirits, ancestors and heroes who inhabit them. How this tradition should play out where Irish religious practices are carried out in non-Irish locations is explored in a poetic example using place-name interpretation and re-interpretation to help heighten the significance of one's local landscape—in the example given, specific locations in Western Washington state and its islands in the U.S.

Onomastic (name-related) and toponymic (placename-related) lore is a rich source for understanding how indigenous peoples have interacted with the lands which they inhabit, and which have shaped their cultures, languages, and religions. Ireland has a long history of—and even an entire genre of medieval literature dedicated to—placenames and the sacred lore associated with them. This interest in toponymy is easily situated within the wider Irish interest in names generally, as exemplified in the Middle Irish text *Cóir Anmann*, "The Fitness of Names,"[1] which details stories about how particular individuals or populations received their names, often having their narrative crux at clever wordplays within the Irish language. This is not a "scientific" study of etymology, but instead is based on the tradition which follows from St. Isidore of Seville's *Etymologiae*, itself a continuation of classical Greek and Roman efforts in the same direction, via which the meaning of names is theorized not from the linguistic study of roots and their cognates across different related languages, but instead is derived from words that have

---

[1] Whitley Stokes (ed./trans.), *"Cóir Anmann," Irische Texte* 3.2 (1891), pp. 285-444; Sharon Arbuthnot, *Cóir Anmann: A Late Middle Irish Treatise on Personal Names*, 2 Volumes, Irish Texts Society Volumes 59-60 (London and Dublin: Irish Texts Society, 2005-2007).

similar morphology (word-forms) or phonology (sounds) as the names in question. Isidore's *Etymologiae* was held in such high regard in medieval Ireland that it was referred to as the *Culmen*, the "culmination" or "sum (of all knowledge)," and in one tale it is even said that the last literary copy of the epic *Táin Bó Cúailnge* was traded to a foreigner for a mere copy of the *Culmen*.[2] Not unlike the great importance of genealogies in Irish literate culture, likewise the importance of placenames in medieval Irish literature reflects what A. Joseph McMullen has referred to as a "genealogy of landscape" for the Irish.[3]

The medieval Irish genre of literature dedicated to placenames is known as *dindshenchas*, "lore of prominent places," from the individual words *dinn* (singular *dú*), "place/location," and *senchas*, "lore/learning." Metrical collections of this lore exist,[4] as well as prose collections from Rennes (in Brittany),[5] Edinburgh (in Scotland),[6] and in Oxford, England at the Bodleian Library.[7] However, this interest in *dindshenchas* is not confined to that specific genre, but is instead found scattered across the entire corpus of medieval Irish literature. In fact, it forms such an important part of the major medieval Irish prose compositions *Táin Bó Cúailnge* (the centerpiece of the Ulster Cycle, featuring the warrior hero Cú Chulainn)[8] and *Acallam na Senórach* (the longest piece of the Finn/Ossianic

---

[2] Tomás Ó Máille, "The Authorship of the *Culmen*," *Ériu* 9 (1921-1923), pp. 71-76.

[3] McMullen's doctoral work on this subject, in the Department of Celtic Studies at Harvard University, is ongoing and will be published in the future, with any luck.

[4] Edward Gwynn (ed./trans.), *The Metrical Dindshenchas*, 5 Vols., Todd Lecture Series 8-12 (Dublin: Royal Irish Academy, 1903-1935).

[5] Whitley Stokes, "The Prose Tales in the Rennes Dindshenchas," *Revue Celtique* 15 (1894), pp. 272-336, 418-484; 16 (1895), pp. 31-83, 135-167, 269-312.

[6] Whitley, "The Edinburgh Dindshenchas," *Folk-Lore* 4 no. 4 (December 1893), pp. 471-497.

[7] Whitley Stokes, "The Bodleian Dindshenchas," *Folk-Lore* 3 no. 4 (December 1892), pp. 467-516.

[8] The text exists in four main recensions, of which only three have been edited/translated. Recension I: Cecile O'Rahilly (ed./trans.), *Táin Bó Cúailnge, Recension I* (Dublin: Dublin Institute for Advanced Studies, 1967). Recension II: Cecile O'Rahilly (ed./trans.), *Táin Bó Cúalnge from the Book of Leinster* (Dublin: Dublin Institute for Advanced Studies, 1968); Cecile O'Rahilly (ed.), *The Stowe Version of Táin Bó Cuailnge* (Dublin, 1978). Recension III: Max Nettlau, "The Fragment of the Táin Bó Cúailnge in MS. Egerton 93 (ff. 26a 1-35b 2)," *Revue Celtique* 15 (1894), 62-78, 198-208; Pádraig Ó Fiannachta (ed.), *Táin Bó Cuailnge The Maynooth Manuscript* (Dublin: Dublin Institute for Advanced Studies, 1980); Feargal Ó Béarra, "Táin Bó Cuailnge: Recension III," *Emania* 15 (1996), pp. 47-65. There are also two commonly-available translations of a mix of recensions I and II available in English: Thomas Kinsella (trans.), *The Tain* (Oxford: Oxford University Press, 1969); Ciaran Carson (trans.), *The Táin* (New York: Viking, 2007).

Cycle, featuring Finn mac Cumhaill and his warriors)[9] that such placename-based concerns may be in large part the *raison d'être* for their composition. This even extends to Welsh tales in the *Mabinogi*, many of which were written with direct Irish influence,[10] and on occasion even give explanations for Irish placenames within their narratives.[11] All of these examples usually reflect the interrelationships of famous persons—whether they be distinguished ancestors, heroes or heroines, deities, other types of supernatural beings, or land spirits (categories with a significant amount of overlap in Irish tradition)—with their landscapes and the significant features of them. Thus, to use McMullen's memorable phrase, they reflect the genealogy of landscape as much as human genealogies reflect the preserved memories of ancestors, and are as important for a deep engagement with sacred land and territory as the names of individual deities are for engaging in divine cultus.

This may be all well and good for someone who lives in Ireland, and who might wonder what mythic significance a particular hill or townland's name may have, thus facilitating their greater engagement with the deities and heroes who came into contact with their localities. But what does this body of literary heritage signify for those who do not live in Ireland, though they may be practicing spiritual traditions which derive from or are inspired by Irish cultures? While there are many towns, cities, streets, and other locations in the United States, Canada, and Australia which might be named after Irish places or persons, the vast majority do not derive from those cultural-linguistic origins, and thus it may not seem relevant nor appropriate to employ such an onomastic methodology of meaning-making on such names.

However, this is not the tradition of the Irish themselves. The interest in language on the part of medieval Irish scholars was promiscuous, and Greek,

---

[9] The text exists in two long recensions (a Middle Irish and an Early Modern Irish version) and a Middle Irish short recension. Middle Irish: Whitley Stokes, "*Acallamh na Senórach*," *Irische Texte* 4.1 (1900), pp. 1-438; translation in Ann Dooley and Harry Roe (trans.), *Tales of the Elders of Ireland: Acallam na Senórach* (Oxford: Oxford University Press, 1999). Early Modern Irish: Nessa Nì ShÈaghdha (ed.), *Agallamh na SeanÙrach*, 3 Vols. (Dublin: Oifig an tSoláthair, 1942-1945). The short recension: Douglas Hyde, "*An Agallamh Bheag*," *Lia Fáil* 1 (1926), pp. 79-107; Walter Pennington, "The Little Colloquy," *Philological Quarterly* 9.2 (April 1930), pp. 97-110.

[10] John Carey, *Ireland and the Grail* (Aberystwyth and Andover: Celtic Studies Publications, 2007).

[11] As, for example, in the Second Branch, the Irish placename of Baile Atha Cliath, "Place of the Ford of Hurdles" (which is the Irish name for the city/area of Dublin), the origin of the name is given narratively as the giant Bendigeidfran lying across the River Liffey, and then hurdles are placed upon him; Patrick K. Ford (trans.), *The Mabinogi and Other Medieval Welsh Tales* (Berkeley and Los Angeles: University of California Press, 1977), p. 67.

Latin, and Hebrew were incorporated into their etymologizing tendencies in such works as *Cóir Anmann and Sanas Cormaic* ("Cormac's Glossary"),[12] and was often extended to names and places that were foreign in origin, including in Britain and further afield. Adomnán of Iona's *De Locis Sanctis* ("On Holy Places"),[13] written in the late 7th century CE—based on the work of the Gaulish monk Arculf—though it is a Christian text about Rome, Jerusalem, and Constantinople's various Christian holy sites, might be an early example of this interest in the significance of particular locations, especially locations of sacred import, and may have reflected a Christianized version of the general Irish interest in place-lore. Thus, for modern polytheists who work within an Irish-derived context, the question becomes: what places are sacred in our own local landscapes, and what kind of word- and name-magic might elevate their significance for our own spiritual engagements?

It must be admitted, this question is one that is highly fraught for many people for a variety of important and very legitimate reasons. There is great fear, for example, that if (as is the case in my own location in western Washington state) a particular river or town has a name derived from a Northwest Coast Native American culture, that such a reinterpretation might result in cultural appropriation. This particular concern is very valid and should loom large for anyone engaging in this kind of work. I personally see the difference in what I am suggesting here and cultural appropriation as being in the nature of what is being borrowed and how it is being portrayed. The placenames that derive from Native American languages are usually Anglicized to varying extents (just as the placenames of Ireland have been Anglicized and often only remotely resemble their Irish originals), thus they may no longer resemble the Native originals in their sound. There is also no question of attributing the new meanings derived from these (or any other) names to the cultures concerned, or using the cultural materials from those peoples improperly or without permission.

When I have discussed these matters with some people whose objections are along the lines above, it has instead been suggested by them that the actual Native American stories of places and peoples be learned, and nothing further be done with them. While I do agree that this is a useful and important set of knowledge to gain (if indeed it can happen—a great deal of these materials have not been recorded), taking these materials from folklorists and academics who have recorded them is also fraught with difficulties. One should not then claim to be an expert in this lore, nor attempt to adapt it to one's own spiritual

---

[12] Kuno Meyer (ed.), *Sanas Cormaic (Cormac's Glossary) Compiled by Cormac Ua Cuilennain, King-Bishop of Cashel in the Tenth Century, Edited from the Copy in the Yellow Book of Lecan* (Felinfach: Llanerch, 1994).

[13] Denis Meehan (ed./trans.), *Adamnán's De Locis Sanctis* (Dublin: Dublin Institute for Advanced Studies, 1958).

culture, because that would be actual cultural appropriation, strictly speaking, quite directly. But likewise, simply learning it and then doing nothing with it seems misguided as well, since it fosters no connections between oneself, one's spiritual practices, and the land one inhabits, nor the indigenous peoples involved, and puts further distance between one's practices and the locations which, in so many ways—from the food grown there to the water which is consumed to sustain our lives—allows us and our deities to survive and thrive in these places, that further alienation seems to be the only possible result.

As has been suggested in relation to cultural appropriation issues and specifically Irish matters elsewhere,[14] what I offer for consideration here is a particularly Irish approach to the question of inhabiting a given land or territory rightfully and ethically in connection with the deities and land-spirits resident within it, which is exemplified in medieval Irish literature itself, and should serve as a model for those interested in these practices. Because Ireland is an island nation and an insular (literally!) culture, and the Irish themselves have no currently known conception of a group of people being truly indigenous to the island—outside of the Fomoiri,[15] perhaps—the Irish understanding of mythological history and their own ancestry involves the notion that successive waves of invaders (some of whom are understood to be genetic descendants of earlier colonial incursions) came to inhabit Ireland and its islands, and to shape the land and name it, generally recorded in the various recensions of the pseudohistorical corpus known as *Lebor Gabala Érenn*, "The Book of the Takings of Ireland."[16] The human population of Ireland is understood, in this context, to be the descendants of the most recent wave of such invaders, all in the family who have as their eponymous ancestor Míl Espaine, whose name

---

[14] Phillip A. Bernhardt-House, "'None May Enter Without Art or Deeds of Heroism': Going Hungry or Whole Hog with Celtic Cultures," in Lupa (ed.), *Talking About the Elephant: An Anthology of Neopagan Perspectives on Cultural Appropriation* (Stafford: Immanion Press/Megalithica Books, 2008), pp. 44-57.

[15] The early Old Irish poem "Mess-Telman" indicates this, as the general inhabitants of the Otherworld and the Fomoiri are not at all distinguished, and the Fomoiri always seem to oppose whatever wave of invaders arrives in Ireland. See John T. Koch (ed./trans.), "Mess-Telman," in John T. Koch and John Carey (eds.), *The Celtic Heroic Age: Literary Sources for Ancient Celtic Europe & Early Ireland & Wales*, Fourth Edition (Aberystwyth and Andover: Celtic Studies Publications, 2003), p. 52.

[16] R. A. S. Macalister (ed./trans.), *Lebor Gabála Érenn, The Book of the Taking of Ireland*, 5 Volumes, Irish Texts Society Volumes 34, 35, 39, 41, 44 (Dublin and London: Irish Texts Society, 1938-1956); the first recension is also translated by John Carey, "The Book of Invasions (First Recension)," in John T. Koch and John Carey (eds.), *The Celtic Heroic Age: Literary Sources for Ancient Celtic Europe & Early Ireland & Wales*, Fourth Edition (Aberystwyth and Andover: Celtic Studies Publications, 2003), pp. 226-271.

literally means "the Spanish soldier," and who are often referred to in commentaries on this material as the Milesians.[17]

Contrary, perhaps, to expectations in this regard, the prominent leader of the Milesians is not a conquering king or warrior, but is instead presented as a superlatively skilled poet (*fili*) and the source of certain important juridical practices in Ireland: namely Amairgen Glúingel ("white-knee") or Glúnmár ("big-knee"). He does not achieve the rightful stewardship of Ireland by any act—whether merely ritualized or literal—of having sex with the Goddess of Sovereignty, as has often been emphasized in writings about Celtic concepts of kingship,[18] but instead through two different means: first, through actual negotiation with the three divine sisters whose names are the eponyms of Ireland itself—Ériu, Fotla, and Banba; and second, through a poetic utterance before symbolically setting foot on the island once again with his party, which begins, "I invoke the land of Ireland…"[19] This methodology for assuming rightful stewardship and lawful habitation of and on the land ends up forcing the Tuatha Dé, the main divine race associated with Ireland, to then inhabit the chthonic otherworld beneath and within Ireland itself, leaving the surface of the island to humans, as is reflected in the *Lebor Gabála Érenn* corpus itself in addition to other tales (e.g. *Mesca Ulad*).[20] Rather than following the precedent of the "King and Sovereignty Goddess" theme so familiar from stories of aspiring kings in Ireland[21] and elsewhere in the culturally Celtic sphere,[22] which

---

[17] Carey, "Book of Invasions," pp. 236, 249-250, 256-257, 263-271; however, rather than following suit with many modern scholars, I think it is a mistake to reify the Milesians as being synonymous with the "Gaelic Irish" who were one of the diverse Celtic peoples that "invaded" Ireland after being pushed to the peripheries of Europe in antiquity, given that there is little to no archaeological evidence that the population native to Ireland is noticeably genetically different from the inhabitants of it whose remains have been recovered from the Paleolithic and Mesolithic periods, and that no appreciable "Celtic invasion" in any large scale or noticeable historical sense has occurred historically.

[18] Proinsias Mac Cana, "Aspects of the Theme of King and Goddess in Irish Literature," *Études Celtiques* 7.1-2 (1955-1956), pp. 76-114, 356-413.

[19] Carey, "Book of Invasions," p. 267.

[20] John T. Koch (trans.), "The Intoxication of the Ulstermen," in John T. Koch and John Carey (eds.), *The Celtic Heroic Age: Literary Sources for Ancient Celtic Europe & Early Ireland & Wales*, Fourth Edition (Aberystwyth and Andover: Celtic Studies Publications, 2003), p. 106.

[21] One of the most prominent examples, often taken as somewhat paradigmatic, is that of Niall of the Nine Hostages; John Carey (trans.), "*Echtra Mac nEchach*: The Adventures of the Songs of Eochaid Mugmedón," in John T. Koch and John Carey (eds.), *The Celtic Heroic Age: Literary Sources for Ancient Celtic Europe & Early Ireland & Wales*, Fourth Edition (Aberystwyth and Andover: Celtic Studies Publications, 2003), pp. 203-208.

are reflective of the concept of *fír flatha*, "ruler's truth,"[23] Amairgen's negotiation and invocation of Ireland through its eponymous goddesses could be seen as a more primal process of poetically-based methodologies of seeking sovereignty and lawful habitation, consistent with a practice and concept known as *fír filid*, "poet's truth."[24]

My suggestions in this regard, then, take into account that as non-natives to North America (though this might apply equally well to people in other non-Irish locations, too), and as polytheistic practitioners especially aware of and sensitive to issues of cultural appropriation, that it will not simply be a matter of finding out the names, placenames and myths of our local indigenous peoples and then reinterpreting or inserting our own ancestors or more modern people (including ourselves!) into them. Instead, with a precedent which will be detailed subsequently, the successive layers of placenames that often are given in Irish texts (in line with the pattern witnessed quite often of characters being re-named in Irish texts as a result of particular actions or occurrences in their lives) will be replicated in how modern Irish-influenced polytheist practitioners come to understand the names of the places where they currently live and practice their religion. There is a town near Oxford in England that was named after the abbey located there, called Abingdon, whose name in Anglo-Saxon means "hill of Æbbe/Æbba," which is likely named after a saint with a church in Oxford now called St. Ebbe's, founded in the late seventh century CE. However, the later medieval Irish authors of the Latin life of the Irish St. Abbán (who lived in the late fifth/early sixth centuries CE) reinterpreted the name as deriving from the Irish saint's missionary activities in England, and it was understood as

---

[22] See the stories from Masilia (Marseille, France) and Galatia, as reflected by the classical authors Athenaeus and Justin, and Plutarch and Polyaenus: John Carey (trans.), "The Foundation of Marseilles," in John T. Koch and John Carey (eds.), *The Celtic Heroic Age: Literary Sources for Ancient Celtic Europe & Early Ireland & Wales*, Fourth Edition (Aberystwyth and Andover: Celtic Studies Publications, 2003), pp. 38-39; John Carey and Philip Freeman (trans.), "The Poisoned Libation: The Love Triangle of Sinatus, Sinorix, and the High Priestess Camma," in John T. Koch and John Carey (eds.), *The Celtic Heroic Age: Literary Sources for Ancient Celtic Europe & Early Ireland & Wales*, Fourth Edition (Aberystwyth and Andover: Celtic Studies Publications, 2003), pp. 40-42.

[23] Calvert Watkins, "*Is Tre Fhír Flathemon*: Marginalia to *Audacht Morainn*" *Ériu* 30 (1979), pp. 181-198.

[24] This is a concept mentioned, but often not further elaborated on, in medieval Irish literature, including Liam Breatnach (ed.), *Uraicecht na Ríar: The Poetic Grades in Early Irish Law* (Dublin: Dublin Institute for Advanced Studies, 1987), pp. 21-24. I hope to return to the interrelation of this concept, as well as *fír flatha* and *fír fer*, "truth of men (i.e. warriors)," in academic publications in the future, and have presented on it at PantheaCon and on other occasions over the past decade.

Abbain dun, "Abbán's fort/town."[25] This Isidorean "etymologizing by puns," so thoroughly Irish (and classically Greek and Roman, for that matter) in its deployment, can easily be applied to the situation with placenames in other lands from other cultural-linguistic origins.

Perhaps what makes this entire process even more interesting is that the reinterpretation or translation of the names of prominent places in our own landscapes will then generate stories—and, this is precisely what happened in the original medieval context, in all likelihood. A name suggests a story, and the names of places were probably long-standing, their etiologies long forgotten, which then were reinvigorated, if not outright reinvented, by extrapolating narratives from punning etymologies which serve to inscribe the landscape with personhood from ancestors, heroes, and deities, as well as the animal, plant, stone, waters, and other divine beings inhabiting or embodying the land. So many features of the land in *Táin Bó Cúailnge* are created from the dismembered parts of the battling bulls, thus inscribing the geography with both narrative and both the history of the magical swineherds-become-bulls as well as all of the symbolic weight of cattle's general importance in the culture as basic units of wealth. Story and name, thus, interplay with each other, and give rise to each other equally. It is a reciprocal process, into which modern polytheists may enter just as certainly as the ancestors of our traditions did in interacting in relationships of reciprocity with land, deities, heroes, and their own ancestors.

I would like to conclude the present investigation and suggestion by offering an example from my own work. In my practice, and that of a Celtic Reconstructionist group with whom I used to collaborate, we celebrated a festival dedicated to Manannán Mac Lir on June 25th each year, honoring the custom of the people of the Isle of Man (named for Manannán) of paying rent to Manannán by making particular offerings of native plants to him on that date.[26] It seemed odd to me, eventually, that we were paying Manannán rent for access to the otherworld through our own locations when there was no attested tradition of him actually inhabiting our own locality; I fully understood and acknowledged that because of his otherworldly connections, we might owe him acknowledgement for our journeys there and thanks-offerings were due to him for safe passage into and out from it, but to assume that this was the case automatically or inherently given our own location in and amongst non-Isle of Man (and non-Irish!) lands and islands, I wasn't sure if this was as wise or sensible as it might have seemed at first glance. Therefore, on this occasion in

---

[25] Charles Plummer (ed.), *Vitae Sanctorum Hiberniae*, 2 Vol. (Dublin: Four Courts Press, 1997), Vol. 1 pp. 12 §14. This folk etymology clearly goes against the usual Irish linguistic practice of having names of this sort in the reverse order, e.g. Dun Ailinne, Dun Óengussa, etc.

[26] Sophie Morrison, *Manx Fairy Tales* (London: David Nutt, 1911), p. 171.

2010, I wrote a poem in English using the methodology suggested above, inviting Manannán to actually inhabit our local sacred places where access to the otherworlds are gained. I present that poem here, with notes indicating how local placenames have been re-etymologized into Irish.

Dán Gabála Manannáin[27]

As it is over nine waves
that Manannán Mac Lir's rulership extends,
it is nine imperfect quatrains
that I offer in his praising:

As you lost your hunting hounds
in Loch Con on a boar's trail,
may Loch Argait be a place
where poets walk dogs in peace.[28]

With Bran's men on their way
to Tír na mBán did you appear;
now appear as the lord of another island,
the Isle of Middle Women;[29]

And as your chariot passed over the waves
easily when you spoke your prophecy to them,
may the ferry at the place called Many Hot-Pigs[30]

---

[27] "Poem of the Takings of Manannan." "Takings" is here understood in the same way as it is in the title of *Lebor Gabála Érenn*, as a "moving into" or "inhabiting of" a particular place.

[28] *Loch Argait*: a literal translation of the name of Silver Lake in south Everett, WA. As I lived in Erynn Rowan Laurie's library at her home on the shores of Silver Lake, and we are both practitioners of *filidecht* and would walk her dog near or around the lake, that is what these lines refer to. As a sacred water source that was significant in my life from mid-2007 to early 2010, when I lived on it and often performed purifications and other practices on or in the lake, it merited recognition. For the story of Loch Con referred to earlier, see Gwynn, Vol. III, pp. 408-409; Stokes, "Rennes" (1894), pp. 474-475; Stokes, "Bodleian," p. 497.

[29] Whidbey Island, .i. *mid* (middle) + *bé* (women). With lenition, the consonant "m" can sound like "w." Whidbey Island is the place where I was born, and where I currently work, and may be moving again in the near future. For the story of Bran and the Isle of Women, see Kuno Meyer (ed./trans.), *The Voyage of Bran Son of Febal to the Land of the Living* (Felinfach: Llanerch, 1994).

[30] Mukilteo, .i. *mucc* (pig) + *il-* (many) + *té* (hot). Mukilteo is a suburb of Everett, and is the place where the ferry from Clinton, WA, on the southern end of Whidbey Island,

always pass safely with passengers.

May the mists in Belach Bréc[31]
not be mists of oblivion
shaken from your cloak at Cú Chulainn,
but be for the memory of *duinebrech*.[32]

Likewise, as over Inis Mán you are lord,
may your sovereignty and protection
extend to the Isle of the Woods of Physicians
where doctors are nurtured amidst forests of letters.[33]

May all who are *cú glas*[34] find
solace near the shores of Loch Belach,[35]

---

meets the mainland. I have traveled on that ferry route innumerable times from my youth, and often used it to commute to work when I lived in Everett. I also wrote poems—including the one to Manannán which can be found on a prayer-card for the deity—while on the ferry or at the ferry terminals in Clinton and Mukilteo.

[31] *Belach Bréc*: "Pass of Deception," a literal Irish translation of Deception Pass, an area and the bridge in it on the north end of Whidbey Island, which is often fog-enshrouded in the morning. The regions on both Whidbey and Fidalgo Islands adjacent to Deception Pass have been sacred locations for me since childhood. It turns out Deception Pass, in addition to its storied history since the time of European occupation, has a supernatural ancestress figure associated with it in the indigenous Samish culture called Kwəkwálǝlwˉt, often known as "the Maiden of Deception Pass."

[32] *Duinebrech*: "Wolf-people," .i. *duine*, "people" + *brech*, an unusual word for "wolf." Because Deception Pass' surroundings have been sacred to me, and I am wolf-identified in some of my practices as well as in my spiritual name, it thus derives this meaning from my own activities as a "wolf-person" in the area. Here, an etymology for Belach Bréc is being given via *brech*; the vowel quality and lenition difference between these forms is inconsequential for the practice of Isidorean etymologizing in Irish. The story of Cú Chulainn's forgetfulness induced by Manannán's cloak is in *Serglige Con Culainn*: Jeffrey Gantz (trans.), *Early Irish Myths and Sagas* (London: Penguin, 1981), p. 178.

[33] Fidalgo Island, .i. *feda* (woods) + *lego* (physicians). *Feda*, singular *fid*, is also the Irish word for the letters of the ogam alphabet. There is a hospital on Fidalgo Island, called Island Hospital, where I have received a lot of medical treatments over the years, including in the aftermath of several near-death experiences I had as a teenager which prompted my involvement in becoming a polytheist, and even when I was a resident on Whidbey Island, the doctors and medical facilities on Fidalgo were much better and often preferred to those more locally.

[34] Literally "grey dog/wolf," but used in legal terminology to mean "outlaw" or "foreigner from across the sea." See Enrico Campanile, "Meaning and Prehistory of Old Irish *Cú Glas*," *Journal of Indo-European Studies* 7 (1979), pp. 237-247.

both fleeing *fénnidi*[36]
and cunning *cáinte*.[37]

May the mountain named for the Cattchennaigh[38]
and the lake of its name beneath,[39]
Loch Cride[40] and the Lake of Battle-Chiefs[41]
be strengthened by you like Éire[42] itself.

As the leash of Núada's hound
was the River Shannon of Connacht and Múman,
may the River of the Shadowy Gate[43]

---

[35] *Loch Belach*: a literal translation of Pass Lake, on southern Fidalgo Island near Deception Pass.

[36] "Warriors of the *Fianna*," identified with werewolves; see Kim R. McCone, "Werewolves, Cyclopes, *Díberga* and *Fíanna*: Juvenile Delinquency in Early Ireland," *Cambrian Medieval Celtic Studies* 12 (1986), pp. 1-22. This carries on the *duinebrech* and *cú glas* imagery.

[37] "Satirist," identified with dogs; see Stokes, "Cóir," pp. 384-385; Arbuthnot, Vol. 2, pp. 64, 137 §249. Again, this carries on the *duinebrech* and *cú glas* imagery, only has further relevance in my own case because of my own activities as a satirist, often performed in the sacred places around that area in order to involve the land and the spirits within it in the actions of turning against the recipients of the satire.

[38] Mt. Erie on Fidalgo Island; it was named after Lake Erie, one of the Great Lakes of the U.S., and Erie itself is a name of a group of people indigenous to the area, which itself means "cat" or "raccoon." As a result, the name has been reinterpreted here to be the name of the Cat-Head people who are often mentioned in Irish literature. Mt. Erie is one of the most sacred locations for me in my local landscape, and thus connecting it via these varied etymologies to the Cat-Heads, and the similarity of this to Welsh traditions connecting a mountain near Edinburgh to Dog-Heads—see Jon B. Coe and Simon Young (eds./trans.), *The Celtic Sources for the Arthurian Legend* (Felinfach, 1995), pp. 130-131—was irresistible to me.

[39] Lake Erie, near Mt. Erie on Fidalgo Island, which is a considerably smaller lake than the Great Lake from whence its name derives!

[40] *Loch Cride*: a literal Irish translation of Heart Lake, also located near Mt. Erie on Fidalgo Island.

[41] A reference to another lake near Mt. Erie, namely Lake Campbell; the surname Campbell is said to derive from the Irish *Cathmhaoil*, "battle-chief."

[42] The name of the modern Republic of Ireland, though it is often misunderstood and mispronounced as "Erie" by Irish Americans, and thus "Erie" is often thought to mean "Ireland." The earliest—relatively informed!—folk etymology of Mt. Erie I ever heard by locals connected it to Ireland in this fashion. Transposition of letters and mispronunciation in order to derive an Isidorean etymology for something in Irish is not unprecedented, either.

gather your people like packs of hounds.

May you reign over sea and shore
and every wave upon the waters
in the Fjord of the Sprites' Gate[44]
for yours is the gate to the Otherworlds.

We are far from Ériu, Alba, and Letha,[45]
far from Dyfet of Manawydan's fame,[46]
far are we from the Isle of Man by many waves,
but may Manannán be welcome in this land as it is.[47]

> P. Sufenas Virius Lupus is a metagender person, and the *Doctor, Magistratum, Mystagogos, Sacerdos*, and one of the founding members of the Ekklesía Antínoou – a queer, Graeco-Roman-Egyptian syncretist reconstructionist polytheist group dedicated to Antinous, the deified lover of the Roman Emperor Hadrian, and related deities and divine figures – as well as a contributing member of Neos Alexandria and a practicing Celtic Reconstructionist pagan in the traditions of *gentlidecht* and *filidecht*, as well as Romano-British, Welsh, and Gaulish deity devotions. Lupus is also dedicated to several land spirits around the area of North Puget Sound and its islands.
>
> *See Lupus' full biographical entry on page 124 of this issue.*

---

[43] Skagit River, .i. *scáth* (shadow) + *geata* (gate). For the association referred to earlier in this quatrain, see Whitley Stokes, "O'Mulconry's Glossary," *Archiv für Celtische Lexikographie* 1.2 (1898), pp. 232-324, at 273.
[44] Puget Sound, which is a very large fjord; .i. *púca* (sprite, troublesome spirit) + *geata* (gate).
[45] The old names for Ireland, Scotland, and Brittany/the Celtic part of the mainland European continent; see John T. Koch, "Ériu, Alba, and Letha: When was a Language Ancestral to Gaelic First Spoken in Ireland?" *Emania* 9 (1991), pp. 17-27.
[46] An area of southern Wales that is the focus of the first and third branches of the *Mabinogi*; it is fairly clear that Manawydan fab Lyr is the cognate of, if not entirely derived directly from, Manannán Mac Lir. See Carey, *Ireland and the Grail, passim*.
[47] The final syllable, word, or phrase of most Irish poems should be a *dúnad*, which is to say it echoes or exactly copies the first syllable, word, or phrase of the poem.

A Typology of Spirits

SARAH KATE ISTRA WINTER

As modern polytheism evolves, spirits need to be given their proper place in devotional practice alongside gods, especially as we strive to localize our religions. To better understand the types of spirits one might encounter in a polytheistic or animistic context, a broad classification is presented. The four categories contain some crossover and gray areas, but comprise a starting point for further discussion.

While great emphasis is placed in modern polytheism on the gods (possibly due to many people being introduced to these traditions via childhood mythology books), the average person in ancient times was likely to have more frequent contact with spirits. Spirits are not only ubiquitous, but they tend to be regarded as more accessible than the pantheonic gods. Moreover, maintaining good relations with the spirits in one's area is crucial to one's success and wellbeing. They can affect climate, fertility (both human and agricultural), personal luck, health, financial stability, and even spiritual development. They facilitate our connection to the natural landscape, and can provide a bridge between ourselves and the gods.

As we struggle to revive and strengthen the old traditions, separated from those roots by thousands of years and often thousands of miles as well, we may at first concentrate on the gods, who are usually considered reachable from any location (not just the place where they were originally worshipped) and therefore universal and adaptable. But in order to put down our own roots and create depth and solidity to our practices, we must place our religion, our worship – even our gods – in the context of the specific *place* where we say our prayers and make our offerings. Polytheism is not complete in a vacuum. It is a complex web of relationships with the divine world, and amongst the most important of these are our interactions with the distinct, unique spirits who surround us. Most of these spirits have at least some attachment to a physical region, and therefore including them gives our religious practices the same important connection to Place that was a key element of all ancient worship, even though the actual places have in some cases changed dramatically.

In furtherance of a greater understanding of the role of spirits within polytheism, I have attempted a loose classification of their many types. What follows is not specific to any one tradition but instead looks for similarities in animistic approaches across cultures and times. There is in fact a lot of gray area and crossover involved here, as many spirits would be attributable to several categories, or perhaps not even fit into any of them, but it seems a good starting point for an ongoing conversation.

1. Spirits of Animals, Plants, Fungi and Minerals
(a) spirits of individual specimens
(b) spirits of an entire species

We start with the spiritual counterparts to the individual physical elements of the natural landscape itself – the flowers, trees, lichen, and toadstools, the birds, fish, mammals and insects, the stones and metals. These generally fall into two categories. In the simplest animistic terms, each and every one of these has a unique spirit, just as each human does – they are all *persons*, whether animate or inanimate, and can be approached as such. While we tend to develop deeper relationships with the less ephemeral of these spirits – the hundred year-old oak tree, the enduring boulder, even a long-lived wild animal periodically encountered over time – we can have potentially meaningful encounters with even a single herb or honeybee. (Some polytheists also develop strong relationships with individual animal spirits through the tending of their physical remnants after death such as pelts, skulls or other bones; these provide a more permanent connection and a place in which the spirit can reside.)

Individual plants and fungi may especially invite spiritual encounters when they are used medicinally or as entheogens. But such use can also put us in contact with the spirit of that whole species, the so-called "Grandfather" spirit. An example would be the spirit of the fly agaric mushroom, experienced by many under its psychoactive influence as an entity known as the Little Red Man. These almost archetypal spirits appear to exist for plenty of other plants and animals as well – one might encounter Oak rather than the spirit of a particular oak tree, or Stag rather than an individual deer, elk or caribou spirit. Some traditions may classify these spirits as gods; the distinction is often a fuzzy one at best.

Obviously making connections with the spirits comprising one's natural surroundings is a crucial first step in localizing one's polytheistic practice. This can be done even in an urban setting – every city has at least a few trees, weeds, wild animals (raccoons, rats, or foxes if you're in England), molds, and of course plenty of insects and rocks.

2. Spirits of Place
(a) spirits of natural or manmade landscape features
(b) genii loci
(c) spirits who live in a specific place and do not leave

Next we look at the "spirits of place" which are tied to larger elements of the landscape. There is a spirit of every significant feature, both natural and manmade. For instance, one can find a spirit of the nearest river, forest, mountain, canyon, lake, swamp, desert, butte, etc., as well as perhaps smaller features such as hills, streams, and ponds. If there are any unusual, noticeable local landmarks – a large erratic boulder, a geyser, a cave – these might warrant special attention. Some spirits can also be connected to human-created landscape features, wells being the most frequently honored in traditional cultures. Other examples include buildings (especially domestic homes, although there's some crossover with a later category), bridges, reservoirs and crossroads.

Sometimes one encounters a *genius loci*, the protective spirit of a specific place that is not necessarily identical to the spirit of the feature itself. In New Hampshire, there is an entity on Mount Washington, referred to locally as "The Presence" and generally feared, which is said to be most active after a recent death on the mountain. Many people, including non-polytheists, will speak of the spirit of a city like Paris or San Francisco, and in Portland, Oregon there is even a depiction of this spirit in the form of a massive statue of a woman holding a trident, called Portlandia.

Finally, there are the individual (although often experienced collectively) spirits who dwell in a specific location and may not be able to leave it – the classic example being the Greek dryads who are bound to their trees. Other Greek nymphs are attached to ash groves, meadows, lakes, marshes and mountainsides. Most if not all polytheistic traditions have similar classes of spirits connected to landscape features – the Slavic spirits of fields, rivers and forests (not to mention bathhouses!), or the many Norse landwights who guard specific homesteads or wild places.

3. The Dead
(a) ancestors
(b) collective dead
(c) solitary or wandering dead
(d) heroes

Honoring the spirits of the dead is a crucial aspect of all polytheistic religions. This can take place on a very personal level, or be approached collectively by a culture or group. The most personal form is obviously ancestor worship, usually of one's biological predecessors but also applicable to those felt to be "spiritual ancestors" – for modern polytheists, this might include the people who originally worshipped our gods or began our traditions.

Some may also honor groups of collective dead, united because they died due to the same event or cause (e.g., veterans of a specific battle or war, victims of a tragedy), or because they are buried in the same place (e.g., the dead of a particular cemetery). These collective dead may have a more direct connection to one's local area than one's ancestors (who are often buried far away), especially the spirits of the local graveyards.

Occasionally one encounters a lone "ghost" – the spirit of a dead person haunting a specific place (sometimes the place they died) or even just passing through.

Finally, there are heroes, to use the Greek sense of the word. These are the spirits of historical or legendary people who have become elevated by a group over time. In Hellenic tradition, they are most often worshipped at their grave site, and therefore most ancient heroes were highly localized. They might also inspire regional cult centers for healing or prophecy. Many were technically figures of legend rather than actual people who lived and died, but they were treated the same. Today, local heroes might include the most famous and loved poets or artists who lived in an area, courageous war leaders, and city founders – as well as characters from folk stories such as Paul Bunyan.

4. Fairies
(a) solitary
(b) trooping

The final category I have selected is also the most nebulous. "Fairies" is an ambiguous term at best, but there is none better that I can find. This category might include spirits such as the Norse *alfar* (elves) and *dvergar* (dwarves), the Gaelic *bean sith* (banshee) and Welsh *ci annwn* (hellhound), and all sorts of goblins, brownies, gentry, white ladies, red caps, etc.

Following Yeats, these are divided into two groups. Solitary fairies live alone, often in wild or abandoned places, and tend to be more mischievous or even malevolent. Trooping fairies are usually experienced collectively, and move from place to place, often seasonally. (The scholar Katharine Briggs delineated a third group, domestic fairies, who tend to appear singly but are more helpful and well-disposed to humans than other solitaries.)

There is obviously a lot of crossover between these sorts of spirits and some of the other categories. For instance, the Slavic *rusalki* are the spirits of young women who died by drowning, haunt a particular body of water, and are generally treated like fairy creatures (they all have green hair, for instance, so they are not simply ghosts of their human selves); they would be classified under 3(c) and 2(c) as well as 4(a). Fairies in general are often conflated with the dead. They are also often closely tied to natural features. And yet, they possess enough unique qualities and quirks (both individually and as collective types) to be considered as a separate category.

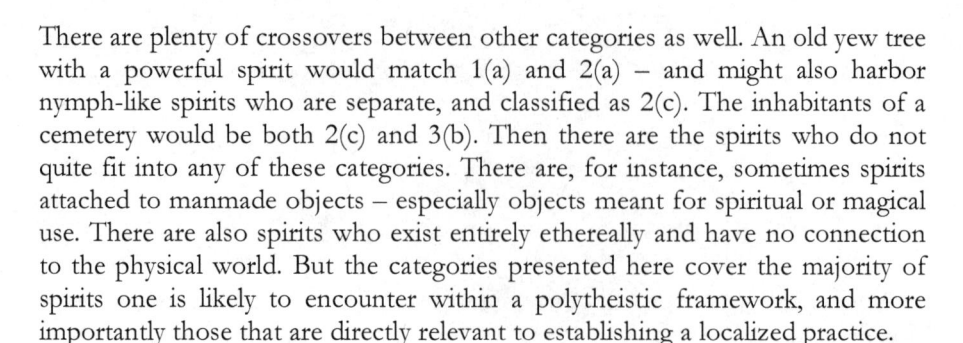

There are plenty of crossovers between other categories as well. An old yew tree with a powerful spirit would match 1(a) and 2(a) – and might also harbor nymph-like spirits who are separate, and classified as 2(c). The inhabitants of a cemetery would be both 2(c) and 3(b). Then there are the spirits who do not quite fit into any of these categories. There are, for instance, sometimes spirits attached to manmade objects – especially objects meant for spiritual or magical use. There are also spirits who exist entirely ethereally and have no connection to the physical world. But the categories presented here cover the majority of spirits one is likely to encounter within a polytheistic framework, and more importantly those that are directly relevant to establishing a localized practice.

Further Reading
Abram, David. *Becoming Animal: An Earthly Cosmology*.
Briggs, Katharine. *An Encyclopedia of Fairies: Hobgoblins, Brownies, Bogies, & Other Supernatural Creatures*.
Dowden, Ken. *European Paganism*.
Gundarsson, Kveldulf. *Elves, Wights and Trolls: Studies Towards the Practice of Germanic Heathenry*.
Harvey, Graham. *Animism: Respecting the Living World*.
Ivanits, Linda J. *Russian Folk Belief*.
Krasskova, Galina. *Honoring the Ancestors: A Basic Guide*.
Larson, Jennifer. *Greek Nymphs: Myth, Cult, Lore*.
Schultes, Richard Evans, et al. *Plants of the Gods: Their Sacred, Healing and Hallucinogenic Powers*.

> Sarah Kate Istra Winter, also known as Dver, is a spirit-worker on the margins of Hellenic polytheism, with ties to English, Germanic and Slavic folk traditions as well. Dedicated to Dionysos, Hermes, and a host of personal and local spirits, her main practices are entheogenic trance, pathwalking, bone-working, sacred art, and devotional worship. Her books include *Kharis: Hellenic Polytheism Explored*, *Dwelling on the Threshold: Reflections of a Spirit-Worker and Devotional Polytheist*, and *Working with Animal Bones: A Practical and Spiritual Guide*. She resides in the lush, green, nymph-haunted Pacific Northwest and blogs at forestdoor.wordpress.com.

Departed Countrymen:
Grave Tending and the Chinese in California

HEATHEN CHINESE

Regional variations of traditional customs are found everywhere, but the experience of being an immigrant in a foreign land tends to produce especially noticeable adaptations. The history of the overseas Chinese in California, especially in small towns such as Santa Cruz, provides interesting examples of this phenomenon with regard to the tending of graves. Because immigrants were often single men without families, the Chinese community historically banded together to make offerings to the deceased. This was a significant departure from Chinese village traditions, where the deceased's family was responsible for such tasks. In Santa Cruz, this tradition was broken with the decline and end of the last Chinatown, but has been revived recently with the help of local historians and the Museum of Art and History. Both in the past and present, tending graves has often involved a complicated relationship with non-Chinese who don't understand Chinese funerary and post-funerary practices, a tension that has parallels in contemporary Hellenic polytheism as well. A crucial component of developing any regional cultus, therefore, is making offerings with enough regularity and consistency that non-practitioners learn to treat sacred spaces with respect.

Ancestor veneration, including the tending of graves, is a central aspect of Chinese culture that supersedes the nominal boundaries of Buddhism, Daoism and popular religion. The Chinese who immigrated to the United States in the 1800s faced two major problems with regard to this traditional obligation. First, they had left the graves of their ancestors behind them. Second, their prospects of having descendants in the United States who would tend *their* graves was slim: in *Chinese Gold: The Chinese in the Monterey Bay Region*, historian Sandy Lydon writes that "[i]mmigration restrictions meant that most Chinese in California (as well as the rest of the United States) were single men who had had to leave their families and had no hope of bringing them to the United States," (130-1). There was little that Chinese immigrants could do about the first problem, but out of necessity, they devised several ingenious solutions in order to address the second.

The first innovation, which made possible all of the others, was for the Chinese community to pool its resources and act as a surrogate family for every one of its members: "for those who had no families, the Chinese organized Benevolent Associations to provide at least some of the missing familial securities and comforts—caring for the indigent and sick, holding funerals, tending graves, and shipping the bones of the dead back to China," (Lydon 131-2). This last "comfort" was one that was rarely necessary in China, but became the favored solution to the problem of being buried in America with no descendants. "A burial brick identifying the deceased and his village of origin was put in the coffin" in preparation for the next step: "within a decade of burial, the body would be exhumed, placed in a box, and shipped back to the family village for final and permanent burial, to be cared for by the deceased's family—forever," (Lydon 132). In other words, most Chinese graves in California were intended as temporary resting places.

Lydon notes that "misunderstood by whites, this [practice] was taken as evidence that the Chinese were mere transients, sojourners" (131), as it was assumed that "the shipment of the dead back to China was another measure of the disdain the Chinese felt for America" (133). Starting in the 1870s and 1880s, California was gripped by a powerful anti-Chinese movement, which was quick to target the practice of exhumation: "In 1878 California passed a law titled, 'An Act to Protect Public Health from Infection Caused by Exhumation and Removal of the Remains of Deceased Persons'," (133). Exhumations still occurred after 1878, but they were tightly regulated and required permits from county health officials.

The Chinese cemeteries underwent exhumations roughly every decade—in the meantime, however, there were still offerings to the dead that needed to be made. The Benevolent Associations took this duty upon themselves as well. Qing Ming, which translates to "Clear Bright," is a festival that occurs fifteen days after the Spring Equinox. Unlike most Chinese holidays, which are calculated according to the lunar calendar, Qing Ming is one of the twenty-four solar terms that farmers used to plant crops by. Traditionally, families would visit and clean the graves of their ancestors on this day. Lydon draws attention to the crucial change to this tradition that occurred in small towns in California: "Where [Q]ing Ming was a family affair in China, it became a community affair in towns like Santa Cruz where the entire Chinese community went out to the cemetery to pay their respects to the spirits of their departed countrymen," (264-5). Not only did the Benevolent Association act as a surrogate for the family during illness and during the funeral, it *continued* to fulfill spiritual obligations to the dead year after year.

The Benevolent Association in Santa Cruz was known as the Chee Kong Tong, for which Lydon relays the translation "Extend Justice Society" (266). The Chee Kong Tong "began as a secret society in seventeenth-century China. Formed to drive the Manchus out of China [...] the society was brought to California by the early immigrants from Canton," (266). The Tong maintained a temple to the warrior god known in Cantonese as Kwan Kung and in Mandarin as Guan Gong or Guan Di (236), and contributed to a sense of cohesion within the Chinese community: "before the 1911 Revolution in China (which rendered some of the tong's political purposes moot), 90% of the Chinese men in Santa Cruz belonged to the Chee Kong Tong; only the Chinese Christians did not join" (268). Chinese converts to Christianity, of course, had no reason to rely upon the Tong in order to have their bones shipped back to China, and could hope to draw upon the resources of non-Chinese Christian missionaries in times of need.

While the vast majority of graves were eventually exhumed, some were not. Lydon comments that "the easiest way to find the Chinese section of a California cemetery (except, of course, the large all-Chinese cemeteries at Colma outside San Francisco) is to walk the perimeter" (266). Santa Cruz is no exception, and there are still at least three Chinese graves at the eastern end of Evergreen Cemetery. One headstone, with only an English inscription, marks the grave of Lee Song (1858-1929). The other two headstones are written in Chinese: I have provided transliterations into Mandarin Pinyin, but the names would be pronounced differently in Cantonese. One headstone marks the grave of "Lin Xian" 林贤 (dates unknown) ; the other marks the grave of a man also surnamed Lin (1851-1926), though a personal name is not readily apparent.

Researchers at the Santa Cruz Museum of Art and History (henceforth SCMAH or the Museum) write that "there were approximately 80 known Chinese buried at Evergreen, we believe we know of 8 remaining individuals," (SCMAH 7). There is also always the possibility of unmarked and undiscovered graves scattered throughout the rural and mountainous areas of the county.

In 2014, the Museum commissioned the construction of a 17-foot tall Chinese Memorial gate at Evergreen Cemetery, in part with funding from businessman George Ow, who grew up in Santa Cruz's last Chinatown. The Memorial consists of a large concrete arch, behind which are five bronze cenotaphs: from left to right, there is one for Yee Lam林义 (d. 1919), one for Chong Lee 李庄 AKA Lue Chong Sing (c.1857-1921), one for Chin Lai AKA Mook Lai Bok or Chen Wenli (d. 1949), one for Lou Sing 娄生 (d. 1884) and one that is blank (SCMAH 1). The blank cenotaph "commemorates all the Chinese buried at Evergreen and in unmarked graves throughout the county," (SCMAH 7). The characters across the top of the Memorial, 圣塔克鲁斯华人常青墓园, translate to "Santa Cruz Chinese People's Evergreen Cemetery." The writing on the vertical columns of the Memorial comprise a two-line poem: the first line of the poem *should* have been inscribed on the right column, so that the poem could be read right-to-left, but unfortunately it was inscribed on the left column instead. The entire poem, 华人先驱奋斗自强/功勋百战流芳万年, roughly translates to: "Chinese pioneers struggled [or fought or strived], to be stronger [or self-reliant]/merit [or honor] was won in a hundred battles, their spirit lasts ten thousand years [i.e. forever]." The Memorial honors *all* of the Chinese who lived and died in Santa Cruz County, but there are some particularly significant "battles" that are represented and honored in the cenotaphs.

Chin Lai's cenotaph is an exact replica of his actual redwood grave marker, which was discovered serving as a floorboard of a children's treehouse near the cemetery, with the Chinese inscription facing downwards. Chin Lai, who worked as a cook in various sawmills and as a vegetable gardener, was the uncle of George Ow, who stated that "We suspect Chen Lai's spirit, who was roaming, made it so that his grave marker was found and could be exhibited [in the Museum]. I see his spirit smiling" (SCMAH 5). Chin Lai's grave marker was used as a model for reconstructing the other three inscribed cenotaphs in as similar a style as possible. Chin Lai's cenotaph occupies the central position of the five, which is an appropriate arrangement given his grave marker's centrality to the process of constructing the Memorial.

Like Chin Lai, Chong Lee (AKA Lue Chong Sing) was also "a Chinese cook well known in different lumber and logging camps," according to his 1921 obituary in the *Santa Cruz Morning Sentinel* (SCMAH 3). Yee Lam's obituary, also printed in the *Morning Sentinel* in 1919, identified him as a laundryman and Chee

Kong Tong member who had served as "the chief mourner to every Chinese funeral" (SCMAH 2). Though his bones were shipped back to China, it is fitting that Yee Lam continues to be honored in the town that he honored and mourned so many others in.

Lou Sing was "a seventeen-year-old Chinese laborer and [Chee Kong Tong] society member" who was found dead in the Santa Cruz Mountains in highly suspicious circumstances in 1884: "Lou Sing had a broken neck and whip marks on his arms," as well as poison in his body (Lydon 269-70). The coroner declared his death a suicide. Though the Chee Kong Tong and the Six Companies of San Francisco hired a surgeon to do another autopsy, which determined that his neck had been violently broken, they were unable to find Lou Sing's murderer. Nonetheless, they "put on the most impressive Chinese funeral in Santa Cruz's history" in order to show "their defiance of the original coroner's verdict," (271). Given the violent circumstances of his death, it is important that Lou Sing's story be remembered and his spirit placated. It is also appropriate that his cenotaph and the blank cenotaph are next to one another, providing connections to the larger historical context with regards to the treatment of the Chinese in Santa Cruz. The *Sentinel* reported in 1884 that Lou Sing's funeral was "also attended by many white people, drawn there by curiosity," (SCMAH 1). One hundred and thirty years later, "many white people" again gathered at Evergreen Cemetery, this time to contribute to memorializing Lou Sing, rather than merely to spectate at his funeral.

Many volunteers, both Chinese and non-Chinese, participated in work parties in order to construct the pathway and steps leading up to the Memorial. Like the Chee Kong Tong before them, the volunteers acted as surrogates for the families of the Chinese men who died alone in America. The Memorial was dedicated on Qing Ming of 2014, and a large crowd of both Chinese and non-Chinese burned incense and "spirit money" as offerings. "Spirit money" is replica paper currency, often with the words "Hell Bank Note" printed on the front (or more recently, "Heaven Bank Note"), that spirits are said to require in the Chinese underworld. Food offerings of oranges were also made in front of the cenotaphs.

As previously noted, the situating of the Chinese section at the extreme edge of the town cemetery is common throughout California, and is a reflection of the exclusion of the Chinese from American society. However, the Chinese are not the only demographic to have experienced exclusion, either historically or in the modern day. One of those other excluded groups is the homeless. Like many affluent small towns in California, Santa Cruz has a vicious track record when it comes to harassing the homeless and driving them out of public spaces. By necessity, a number of homeless individuals end up spending time in and around Evergreen Cemetery. Since the Chinese section of the cemetery is far away from the road and prying eyes, it tends to be one of the spots that people gravitate toward.

Historically, the relationship between the Chinese and destitute non-Chinese in Santa Cruz was a rather strange one. Sangye Hawke, Evergreen Volunteer and Historical Researcher at SCMAH, wrote that food offerings at funerals were often removed and eaten by non-Chinese: "When the main funeral cortege had left, those remaining non-Chinese spectators would often partake in the remnants of the meal. In a way, this living action personified the idea of hungry ghosts. Thefts of funeral food offerings continued into the 1920s," (Hawke). Though in Chinese culture, food offerings made at home shrines are often eaten afterwards by those who made the offering, and many families have a picnic at or near the cemetery on Qing Ming, for non-Chinese spectators to eat food that has been placed at a grave is another matter. Many Chinese traditions are extremely cautious—some would say superstitious—about all forms of conduct in graveyards. For example, I was taught to go to a store or marketplace after visiting the cemetery, rather than returning home directly, so that any ghosts that might be following me would get lost in the crowd. Given this context, I personally feel that eating food that has been offered and left exposed in a cemetery is not the wisest idea, especially for people who had no part in making the offering and therefore have no established positive relationship to the spirits to whom the food was offered. Perhaps the non-Chinese spectators were driven to take food from the graves out of necessity; however, their actions still betrayed a lack of understanding and respect for traditional Chinese customs.

There has been a somewhat similar debate within Hellenic polytheism about the difference between food offerings to chthonic entities and charitable gifts to the poor. In her essay "Hekate's *deipnon*," Dver explains that "the *deipnon* ("dinner" – plural *deipna*) is an offering left at a crossroads on the dark moon (the last day of the lunar month, by ancient Greek reckoning) for Hekate and the spirits of the dead in Her company" (Dver). She notes that traditional and modern practices around the *deipnon* have diverged dramatically:

> Conventional wisdom is that one should leave these offerings and then walk away without looking behind them. The whole offering is left for Hekate; the meal is <u>not</u> shared as in most Greek sacrifices. For years in the modern Hellenic polytheist communities, a misconception has been floating around about the idea of the *deipnon* having been a roundabout way to feed the poor. This has become so prevalent that many people are now donating to homeless shelters and food banks <u>in lieu of</u> making proper *deipna*, and that's something I'd like to see changed. (Dver)

Dver goes on to note that the basis for the modern practice is a single line—intended as mockery, not as description of a deliberate religious practice—in the play *Plutus* by the comic playwright Aristophanes, and argues that calling a donation to the poor by the same name as Hekate's *deipnon* "is potentially problematic – in that if you offer food on Hekate's night, in Her name, but someone else receives and consumes that food, they are unknowingly partaking of an offering that should have rightfully been exclusively reserved for the goddess, and may suffer ill-effects from such," (Dver). In his essay on the same topic, "Stercus olet foedum, quo plus vertendo movetur," Sannion makes a similar point about the potentially disastrous consequences of eating food that has already been given as an offering to Hekate:

> I mean, if you call this donation Hekate's *deipnon* then that means that you are consecrating it to the vengeful spirits of the crossroads, as our ancient Greek predecessors did. And now some unlucky bastard has just been given it to eat. But on the other hand, he *has* chosen to eat the accursed food of his own free will, marking him as lawful prey of the hounds of Hekate, so if something horrible comes for him in the night he's really only got himself to blame. (Sannion)

A similar tension and danger arises in the context of Chinese grave offerings. Sangye Hawke makes an extremely interesting point about the possibility that actions such as removing food from graves actually "personified the idea of hungry ghosts." A "hungry ghost" is syncretic Buddhist-Daoist-folk religion concept of a spirit who has died without proper burial rites, without descendants who will honor them or under particularly unpleasant (especially violent) circumstances. In *The Lunar Tao*, Deng Ming-Dao writes that "if a person dies without a family or if the family is not devout, then that person becomes a hungry ghost—an abandoned spirit with no one to feed it," (Deng 230). Like Tantalus in Greek mythology, hungry ghosts are doomed to eternal hunger and thirst. In a sense, the condition of the homeless in Santa Cruz is not dissimilar to that of the hungry ghost in the spirit world—both have difficulty meeting their basic needs due to their abandonment by, and exclusion from, mainstream society. In his essay "Death & Supper," also addressing the debate around Hekate's *deipnon*, Jack Faust draws a similar connection between the restless dead associated with Hekate and the homeless both of ancient Greece and modern California:

> The poor – particularly the homeless – were less likely than those of other classes to have proper funerary arrangements made for them. In fact, one might argue that the homeless are amongst those most predisposed to ending up in the ghastly condition of restlessness after

death. The homeless already live amongst the restless dead, side-by-side. While I won't argue that California is even remotely similar to areas of Greece in antiquity, I have personally observed the homeless in my city sleeping just outside – and if it is raining, occasionally inside – local cemeteries. (Faust)

If someone is already at risk of becoming a "hungry ghost" or joining the "restless dead," perhaps that threat loses much of its power to dissuade actions such as eating food intended for the dead. On the other hand, physically personifying a "hungry ghost" through one's actions is likely to significantly increase the risk of becoming one. Ultimately, people will make their own decisions, but it is important for polytheists to consider the elaborate chains of consequence that will inevitably follow.

I've never noticed removal and consumption of food offerings in the years I've visited the Chinese graves and Memorial in Evergreen Cemetery. Hopefully, that particular practice no longer occurs. However, I *have* seen an incense burner that I placed at the Memorial mysteriously emptied of sand, containers of incense sticks removed repeatedly and copious amounts of trash strewn around the Memorial. While the former two phenomena could have a variety of strange explanations, the latter is clearly a sign of lack of respect. I also once met a man who was lying on the ground in front of the cenotaphs with his private parts exposed, while incense sticks were *still smoking* in the burner. I explained to him that the Memorial is a sacred space, and that he should treat it "as he would a church." He acknowledged that he could tell that "something ceremonious" was going on, apologized for being unaware of its religious significance and offered to leave. I replied that I wasn't telling him to leave the cemetery, merely to be respectful of the Memorial.

I relate these anecdotes *not* to further the anti-homeless narrative already dominant in Santa Cruz (and in too many other cities), but to point out that polytheist practice often still occupies—and is forced to share—the most liminal physical spaces in a given region. Of course, cemeteries will *always* be liminal spaces, and polytheists will *always* honor their dead, so this particular situation cannot be avoided. Nor should it be. Dealing with the scars and still-open wounds of local history, navigating the ongoing class and social tensions of the towns one lives in, struggling to establish respect for sacred spaces on a *material* level – all of these are important components of developing regional cultus. As the early Chinese immigrants in Santa Cruz knew, it is vital to continue making offerings, despite whatever challenges one might face.

A story from Oakland, California illustrates the power of regular practice in delineating spaces as sacred. A man named Dan Stevenson installed a Buddha statue at the end of a cul-de-sac in 2009. Stevenson explains that the initial changes he noticed were minor: "The Buddha sat there for several months and slowly we noticed slight changes in the garbage environment. The garbage and mattresses didn't stop arriving but the dumping occurred on the other end of the street divide from where Buddha sat" (Stevenson). Over time, people began leaving offerings of fruit, flowers and incense in front of the statue. "For a long time," Stevenson writes, "I did not see anyone bringing the offerings. They just appeared. Along with all this new activity the area continued to change and the illegal dumping all but disappeared. Many neighbors started to pick up and clean the area more. And due to people being present at different times of the day the drug and urination problem ended," (Stevenson). Eventually, a beautiful wooden shrine was constructed by a Vietnamese man who lived in the neighborhood. The *San Francisco Chronicle* reported in 2014 that within a one-block radius of the shrine, "Since 2012, when worshipers began showing up for daily prayers, overall year-to-date crime has dropped by 82 percent. Robbery reports went from 14 to three, aggravated assaults from five to zero, burglaries from eight to four, narcotics from three to none, and prostitution from three to none," (Johnson). When this story is told with the assumption of a secular worldview, there is a very real danger of reinforcing pro-gentrification political discourse. From a polytheist religious worldview, however, this story speaks of the importance of making regular offerings if one wishes to see one's sacred spaces respected.

As the Memorial poem at Santa Cruz's Evergreen Cemetery states about the Chinese in Santa Cruz, through the merit that "was won in a hundred battles, their spirit lasts ten thousand years." How can those living today do any less than those who came before? Like the Chinese in Santa Cruz, modern day polytheists must find ways to adapt to their severance, however great in geography or time, from traditional social structures that were conducive to fulfilling religious obligations. In studying local history, one might find historical precedents which are echoed in modern practice, such as the idea of "surrogate family" tending Chinese graves in Santa Cruz in the 19th century as well as the 21st. What *kinds* of adaptations to make to traditional practices, and which *particular* strands of history are appropriate to draw from, will of course vary greatly from locality to locality. The inherent complexity of polytheism demands nothing less.

Works Cited

Deng Ming-Dao. *The Lunar Tao: Meditations in Harmony with the Seasons*. New York: HarperOne, 2013. Print.

Dver. "Hekate's *deipnon*." *A Forest Door*, 29 June 2011. Web. 8 Apr. 2015.

Faust, Jack. "Death & Supper." *Dionysian Atavism*, 3 Dec. 2013. Web. 8 Apr. 2015.

Johnson, Chip. "Buddha seems to bring tranquility to Oakland neighborhood." *San Francisco Chronicle*, 15 Sep. 2014. Web. 12 Apr. 2015.

Hawke, Sangye. "Stairway to Heaven." Santa Cruz Museum of Art and History, 2014. Web. 11 Mar. 2015.

Lydon, Sandy. *Chinese Gold: The Chinese in the Monterey Bay Region*. Capitola: Capitola Book Company, 1985. Print.

Sannion. "Stercus olet foedum, quo plus vertendo movetur." *The House of Vines*, 14 Nov. 2013. Web. 8 Apr. 2015.

Santa Cruz Museum of Art and History, Evergreen Research. "Chinese Memorial Headstone Information." Apr. 2014. PDF File.

Stevenson, Dan. "Saving Oakland's 'favorite' Buddha." Oakland Local, 2012. Web. 12 Apr. 2015.

> Heathen Chinese is the son of Chinese immigrants. He is a diasporic Chinese polytheist living in the San Francisco Bay Area (stolen Ohlone land). He practices ancestor veneration and worships (among others) the warrior god Guan Di, who has had a presence in California since the mid-1800s. He writes at godsandradicals.org and at heathenchinese.wordpress.com.

Adventures in Active Listening: Connecting to the Neighborhood

VIRGINIA CARPER

Many people often think that a practice of regional *cultus* can only be done in natural areas. However, developing such a practice can be accomplished anywhere. It starts simply by taking daily walks around the neighborhood. Stopping to notice the plants and animals furthers that bond to the area. A deeper connection is then fostered by studying the natural history of the area, and applying that knowledge on the walks. By "actively listening" to the Spirits who live there forges the bond between Them and the person. Living in an urban region dominated by the tracks of the Norfolk and Southern Railroad, Virginia Carper used these methods to create a regional *cultus* of her home. This essay details her efforts and methods in a series of adventures with the Spirits of the Land. Beginning with her walks to the garbage dumpsters, she came to know the Beings of her neighborhood. Eventually, she met the "Head" Spirit of the Land, who was the Being of the Railroad Cut. In retelling her adventures, Carper came to realize that the local Beings are waiting for humans to come and listen to Them. By "active listening," people offer their selves, thereby establishing the bonds of hospitality and reciprocity, necessary for a *cultus* to continue.

Although I live in an urban area by the railroad tracks, I am surrounded by nature. Various plants and animals have adopted this unnatural place, whilst others remain from ages past. The oak and maple trees behind my garden condo shade my small balcony. The local woodpeckers like to drum on the gutters at daybreak, waking everyone up. Of course, there are the squirrels, who nest in the trees. A little intermittent stream appears when it rains between the two garden condo buildings. The rocks, lining the stream, provide places for snakes to sun themselves.

As I go about my daily activities, I often pay attention to what is going on around me. I watch the squirrels bury their nuts, and the robins feast on small cherries. In noticing small things such as mushrooms sprouting after a soaking rain or the local woodchuck peeking out of his burrow near the railroad tracks, I realized the truth of the saying, "The world is so full of a number of things, that we should be as happy as kings." Thus began my adventures in active listening to the Spirits of the Land.

Active Listening

What is "active listening?" To me, it means listening with not only your ears but also with your heart, as well. At their website, the U.S. Department of State give "Four Rules of Active Listening."

1. Seek to understand before you seek to be understood.
2. Be non judgmental.
3. Give your undivided attention to the speaker.
4. Use silence effectively.

When actively listening, it is important to remain silent and focus on the wholeness of the other person. Be patient and attentive. Focus on the concepts, details, and ideas that are being conveyed. Afterwards, always reflect on what was said and unsaid.

Since I was already paying attention, I guess that the next step for me was to be patient and silent. Meanwhile, I would study the natural history of where I lived. A part of active listening for me was knowing about who I was talking to. Furthermore, I always use the taxonomic nomenclature when referring to the plants and animals, since it is important to know their actual names. Over time, with repeated visits to various places in my neighborhood, I came to know the "Spirits of the Land," who lived there. Because active listening requires your full self, I realized that it was a way to honor these Beings.

While I was learning to actively listen, whenever I encountered an animal, I would stop and try to "commune" with it. Meeting a garden snake (also known as "garter," (*Thamnophis sirtalis*, Family Colubridae) on the steps of the common laundry building, I focused on quietly breathing with Garden Snake. After a while, I could see life at her level. We conversed about the warm sunshine and the local rat population.

On a warm September morning, I watched the Green Darners (*Anax junius*, Family Aeshnidae) at the wood's edge by the railroad tracks. They were migrating south. Standing silently, I observed Them eating insects on the wing. When a "Dragonfly" alit on the rail fence, I started breathing with It. Breathing in unison, I could see the Green Darner, glowing in hues of bright green, in my mind's eye.

What I learnt by attending to the animals is that there is a world beyond humans and their activities. By being aware and still, I could "commune" with various animals. With a respectful attitude, I could experience their world as they did. This is the first step in connecting to the Beings of my neighborhood.

Listening to Plants

Following my success with the local animals, I next tried to listen to the plants. Whenever I passed by the forsythia bushes near my condo building, I could sense their "spirit." As I did with the animals, I first studied the natural history of these bushes. Afterwards, I read about any "magical qualities" that these plants may possess. Then I went out on many spring and summer days and "communed" with Them.

Forsythia (*Forsythia x intermedia*, Olive Family)

According to *"Heal Yourself with Flowers and Other Essences"* by Nikki Bradford, the essence of Forsythia can be used to help people with their addictions. The author writes that this plant can give a person the strength to change their engrained habits. From the book, *"Allow the golden yellow of my blossoms to bathe you in the light of transformation. Let me strengthen your willingness to move forward."*

The natural history of the Forsythia does suggest this particular attribute of its magical qualities. Brought from China in 1842 by Robert Fortune (famous plant explorer), this bush (*Forsythia viridissma*) thrived unexpectedly well in both England and North America. Robert Fortune named the plant after William Forsyth, who had started the Royal Horticultural Society of Great Britain.

Before that in 1833, another species of Forsythia (*Forsythia suspensa*) had been introduced in Europe as a lilac. After further taxonomic work, botanists decided it that was a new genus of the Olive Family (*Oleaceae*), and classified it with the Forsythia Genus (*Forsythia*). Since that time, this plant has mutated several times, providing gardeners with a variety of choices, such as being more upright or having larger flowers. Forsythia demonstrates the ability to start over fresh.

Often seen as one of the first signs of spring, the bright yellow flowers of the Forsythia Bush shouts, "SPRING IS COMING!" Walking down a drab street on a cold, grey day, a person feels often happy after seeing this cheerful bush. Its flowers give hope and reassurance that warm weather is soon to arrive. Like Forsythia, we can be bright on the greyest day, knowing that a better day is coming.

Forsythia is a brave shrub. Whilst many plants wait for warmer weather, Forsythia pops out, in cold March, in all its glory. A person can draw strength from the courageous saffron flowers of this plant.

People frequently plant this shrub because It is adaptable to many conditions. Few diseases can attack a forsythia bush. It is easy to reproduce either by cuttings or by pruning It back. In addition, the shrub will root Itself by drooping branches on the ground. Later, these branches will root on the spot.

People also like Forsythia because It acts as a living wall or a privacy fence. When this bush is leafed out, It forms a dense screen. Forsythia shields people from unpleasant things, and offers privacy.

With its vigorous growth, one forsythia bush can overrun a large area. According to horticultural experts, in five years, a shrub can grow eight feet tall (nearly three meters) and five feet across, (almost two meters.) Because of this ease in taking over an area, It is often listed as an invasive plant species. Unless Forsythia is carefully monitored, It can crowd out native plant species. The shadow side of Forsythia is its heedless dominance.

These aspects of Forsythia help me to understand its relations with the Fairies. The Bush provides places for the Fairies and other Nature Spirits to dance. Forsythia protects Them from view, and offers Them shelter.

In this aspect, Forsythia acts as a gateway to the Otherworlds. If you stand quietly on a bright spring day, you can see the Fairies come and go. Also on quiet summer evenings, the Nature Spirits peer shyly from underneath the leaves. This ordinary plant keeps secrets well.

Forsythia helps people to understand that they can grow where they are planted. They can be transformed into something better. Be brave and go out into the cold world to bring happiness is what Forsythia counsels us. However, always be aware the shadow side of Forsythia – excessive and overwhelming force. As we do with the Fairies, we must also approach Forsythia with caution. This bush's good qualities must be tempered with moderation.

White Oak (*Quercus alba*, Beech Family)

After my conversations with Forsythia, I prepared to actively listen to the trees. Again, I studied the natural histories of the trees in my area, and researched any magical properties they may possess. Since it was the middle of winter when I started, I waited for a "January thaw day."

Behind my garden condo is a small stream with a grove of trees. My balcony faces an ancient Twin White Oak (*Quercus alba*, Beech Family), a member of this grove. In fact, this oak's branches extend to the roof of my building. This tree consists of two males who often finish Each Other's sentences. Since the Twin White Oak has been my friend for many years, I thought we could have a quiet conversation.

On this day, They were sleepy, having just woken up for the warm day. Devoid of leaves, the Twin White Oak's branches swayed in the slight breeze. Nuthatches were searching for bugs on the trunk, while the titmice were flitting from branch to branch. A flock of geese flew overhead, honking a greeting to the tree. Sleepily, the Twin White Oak acknowledged the calls of the Canada geese.

A few days before a storm had blown through taking with it, the large squirrel nest from the main branches of the Twin White Oak. Upset at this,

They felt sad that the squirrels had to build a new home elsewhere. Since They were asleep at the time, the Twin Oak could not save the nest. Regarding Themselves as a protector of life, They wanted the squirrels to feel secure with Them.

As I sat with the Twin White Oak, a squirrel jumped up on a branch near my balcony. The upset animal angrily "cheeed" at me, screaming that I was bothering the Twin White Oak. Before the Twin White Oak settled back down to their slumber, They said that the squirrels do like to guard them. This particular squirrel (Cut Ear) warned me not to disturb the Tree again. I have no idea what this squirrel would do to me, but I certainly did not want to find out. So I went inside.

Other Trees

In my listening to various trees, I discovered that every species is so dissimilar from the others that the word "tree" is too general to describe these Beings. The Basswoods acted as a community while the Tulip Poplar stood tall by Herself. Meanwhile the local Scarlet Oaks did not regard Themselves as Kings of the Forest, but preferred to play with everyone instead.

The American Basswoods (*Tilia americana*, Linden Family) live near the railroad tracks behind my condo building. They all wanted to speak to me but only the Younger Brother was in a place where I could safely go. The Basswoods asked me to greet all of them, which I complied by touching their leaves. (The Basswood Community, for some reason, felt male, both separately and together.) Standing together, these trees formed a shady bower with their curved trunks and branches. While I stood in the bower that the trees formed, I could hear music. The Basswoods were singing, in various harmonies, the pop music of Barry Manilow (American, 1943 -). The choral singing of these trees reminded me that I could be an individual within a unified whole, since the Basswoods, Themselves, were a community who relied on each other.

Later, the ancient huge Tulip Poplar (*Liriodendron tulipifera*, Magnolia Family) informed me that She was the Monarch of the Forest. Standing tall, scraping the sky, She told me that She saw the original railroad being laid down in the 1850s. The Tulip Poplar, most decidedly a She, wanted me to know that. As the Reigning Empress, She ordered me to stand tall and stretch to the sky, while keeping my balance. Because I balked at this, the nearby trees told me to hush and listen to Tulip Poplar. After that, I was with Monarch Tulip Poplar for a long time, just standing still. From Her, I learned to be quiet and still.

When the Scarlet Oak (*Quercus coccinea*, Beech Family), who lived near the dumpsters, found out that I was making the rounds visiting trees, He/She dropped several acorns on me. Usually when I drop off my trash, I would visit with that particular Scarlet Oak. This quiet tree wanted me to play with Her/Him. (For some reason, the Scarlet Oak wanted me to know that She/He was both male and female.) We played "acorns" for a while until the two nearby Scarlet Oaks decided to join in the game. Feeling contented and full of fun, the Scarlet Oaks and I threw acorns at each other, while. The Scarlet Oaks informed me that They were not rulers of the forests here, but that the Tulip Poplar and Sycamore were. The Scarlet Oaks were contented to live in the shade of the taller Sycamores. My friend, the Scarlet Oak wanted me to laugh, and to experience wanted me to laugh, and to experience joy in my life. I shall continue to visit He/She and play.

Listening to the Spirits of the Land

At The Dumpster

Following my experiences with the Trees, I decided to try to hear the other Spirits of the Land. Early each Sunday morning, I take my trash out to the dumpster near my building. Behind this dumpster is a large field bordered by woods. Beyond the woods are the railroad tracks of the Norfolk and Southern Railroad. Since everything seems so still at this time, I often go to the edge of the woods to listen to "morning."

The Sunday, I focused on "actively listening to day break" was a winter day, devoid of greenery. I stood at the edge of the woods and awaited the day to begin, which out started grey and overcast. The sun was rising but the light was still low. First, I heard the "coo, coo, coo" of the mourning doves, who were resting in the maple trees. The red-bellied woodpecker, hopping along on a trunk of an oak tree, answered them with "Churrups, churrps." A staccato rhythm continued with the doves and woodpecker calling and responding.

While that was going on, two Carolina wrens searched for food among the tangled basswood trees, hopping from limb to limb. Finally stopping, they began to trill loudly, "pidaro, pidaro, pidaro." These small pugnacious birds provided the counterpoint to the doves and woodpecker. The rhythm of the bird calls became faster and faster, announcing "Morning is coming!"

Then silence came abruptly over the field. Something unseen had passed through the woods. My grandmother referred to this phenomenon of noise then sudden silence as "an angel just walked by." In the presence of the Sacred, we all became silent.

After a brief while, the woodpecker quietly went "quir, quir." Then, the two wrens answered, with "tweepudo dip dip dip." Adding to their calls, the doves boomed "coo, coo, coo." Again the rhythm of the doves calling and the other birds responding continued, as if nothing had happened. Once the sun became brighter, the birds stopped and went about their business. Morning had arrived.

At The "Swamp"

Reflecting on my dumpster experience, I ventured to other places to discover more about the Spirits of the Land. I decided to go to a liminal place at a "between" time. I walked to a swampy area where three streams converge. On two sides of this area are woods, several houses on one side, and a road on another side. Crossing over the swamp was a bridge spanning the road and the houses on the hill. This is a liminal place for me for several reasons, such as the swamp is neither earth nor water. Moreover, the wild area lies between a road and houses, with the bridge connecting the two.

For me, noon represents mid-life followed by old age. After the noon hour comes the afternoon, the decline of the day. Since noon, for me, is the "hinge" of the day, I chose this hour to start to meditate on "old age." I wondered if the experience at the dumpsters would happen again.

The day I went was a blustery winter day. The strong wind blew the dried leaves, which swirled around me, in small eddies. Meanwhile, the sparkling stream water, as it rippled over the tangled roots, reflected the weak winter sun. Seeing the dead leaves strewn about the bottoms of bare trees, I was reminded of "old age." As the sharp wind knifed through me, it called to mind my own mortality. Moreover, I was off the beaten path, in a place of ancient decay, symbolic of "old age." The active life, represented by the road and houses, was separated from me by this swamp.

As I stared out at the swampy overgrown area, an ancient Being of hoary old age popped out of the bog. This male Being had an unkempt appearance with unruly white hair sticking out of his brows and ears. Sailing about on the wind, He played with the whirling leaves. Laughing, the being said to me, "Never be neat, clean, or civilized. Always be wild and unruly. Never be staid or docile." As I listened, the Being twinkled at me and danced off.

As I was leaving, I felt the wildness of the swamp bubble up inside of me. Being old was a time to not to live up to anyone's expectations, instead it was a time to be content with myself. The Being's advice had resided inside of me, and made me rethink growing old. I think I should go and play in the gusting wind with wild abandonment.

At the Railroad Cut

After this profound experience, I realized that I had to do much more than to simply wander around my neighborhood. I needed to introduce myself to the "Head" Spirit of the Land and make offerings. To speak to the "Head" Spirit of the Land, I went to the nearby railroad cut. On one side of the tracks was a small park and on the other side, a large park with a man-made lake. A pedestrian bridge crossed over the tracks to connect the two parks. Running through my neighborhood, the railroad is a constant presence in our lives. Meanwhile, the Land Spirits have accepted the railroad and often use it to connect with people.

When I arrived at the small park, I asked to be received by the Spirits of the Land. While walking the path to the bridge, I gloried in the first day of Spring.

It was a warm day, whispering of life ready to reappear. As I approached the bench by the bridge, a robin hopped out of the woods into the clearing. Cocking its head towards me, the bird trilled a melody. I was welcomed by the Spirits of the Land.

While sitting at the bench, soaking up the warm sun, I waited for a Being to speak to me. Then freight train rattled on through bringing with it, the Being of the Cut. Apparently this ancient Being enjoyed playing with the trains. The Being also like watching people crossing the bridge back and forth.

The Being of the Cut first noticed people when they blasted into its hill many years ago. Curious, It approached the workers and were told that they were Irish. The workers regarded the Being as one of "Sidhe," although It did not know what that meant. However, the Being did like that the workers always respectfully greeted It. Afterwards, the Being became more kindly disposed to people and their trains.

The Being of the Cut told me that It knew me, and regarded me as an old friend. For many years, I would come in the Spring to look for the bluets, growing amongst the moss on the rocks at the cut. I also would search for the white and yellow violets later on. The Being enjoyed my delight at finding these little flowers. As the Being told me this, It settled around me like an old favorite blanket, cozy and warm.

After a while, I asked for a token of our bond. Confused, the Being said, "Are not the bluets and violets, which are soon to bloom, enough?" Embarrassed, I apologized for presuming too much. Sitting for a while longer, I wanted to make sure that the Being was not disappointed in me.

Walking up the path to the road, I was surprised by a Promethea silk moth, a large black moth with gold-silver trim. The moth danced in front of me and showed off its gold-silver tips. Then a second one came and the two tangoed higher and higher up through the trees. I was witnessing a mating dance. Then one of the moths returned to rest on the ground, next to my feet. A few minutes later, the moth flew around me, glimmering in the sun. After that, it flew off to rest in the nearby leaf litter.

I realize that the Being wanted me to return and spend more time in its company. To the Being, I was a friend. We had shared in the joy of the first day of Spring. Leaving, I felt whole, and eagerly waited for the bluets to appear.

Conclusion

Walking home, I realized that by actively listening to the animals, plants, and other beings in my area, I had developed a regional *cultus*. Since I lived in the same place for years, I intimately knew the natural features of my home. Because I always found something enchanting, I enjoyed my walks to the dumpster, the park, the "swamp," and other places. By taking delight in small things, I had earned the respect of the Spirits of the Land.

My regional *cultus* started when I noticed the natural world outside my door. It developed further when I returned to the same places to discover more amazing things. Through my efforts at active listening, I deepened my *cultus*. My activities taught me that the Beings are waiting for us to hear Them. Because active listening requires the gift of my self, the Spirits of the Land found this to be an acceptable offering to Them.

By walking daily and listening actively, I now have an appreciation of my neighborhood and my place in it. I have developed a reciprocal relationship with the Spirits of the Land. I give Them traditional offerings, but active listening is the offering They want the most.

Works Used

----, "Active Listening." U.S. Department of State. Web. http://www.state.gov/m/a/os/65759.htm. <accessed 11 March 2015>.

Bradford, Nikki, *"Heal Yourself with Flowers and Other Essences."* Quadrille Publishing Ltd: London. 2006. Print.

Hageneder, Fred, *"The Meaning of Trees."* Chronicle Books: San Francisco. 2005. Print.

Hidalgo, Sharlyn, *"The Healing Power of Trees."* Llewellyn: Woodbury MN. 2010. Print.

Hopman, Ellen Evert, *"A Druid's Herbal of Sacred Tree Medicine."* Destiny: Rochester VT. 2008. Print.

---, "Listening Skills." Skills You Need. 2015. Web. http://www.skillsyouneed.com/ips/listening-skills.html. <accessed 11 March 2015>.

Wells, Diana, *"100 Flowers and How They Got Their Names."* Algonquin Books of Chapel Hill: Chapel Hill, NC. 1997. Print.

Virginia Carper, a Roman Polytheist, lives in the Washington D.C. area with her family. She is a Dedicant (Roman Hearth) of ADF. Majoring in Divination and Minoring in Lore, She is a Level 5 Student at the Grey School of Wizardry. She has published articles in ADF's *Oak Leaves* and *Walking the Worlds*. Her writings can be found at her blog: *Nature: Observations and Meanings* (naturemeanings.blogspot.com).

The Lobsterman of Portland, Maine: Urban Cult Objects in a Heathen Context

WAYLAND SKALLAGRIMSSON

Ancient heathen practice put as much, if not more, emphasis on local spirits as on pantheonic gods. Some of these spirits can easily be found in urban environments by identifying objects, such as statues, that receive significant local attention and even offerings by pagans and non-pagans alike. Paying cult to such spirits results in a unique, regional form of heathenry that is consistent with the variation found in the ancient religion.

A few years ago I returned to the city of Portland, Maine, for the first time since the nineties. One of the first things I did was head to the square in front of the old Nickelodeon Theater and pay my respects to the Lobsterman. Portland is an old fishing city, and most Maine lobster is caught by boats that put out of a Portland harbor. To honor the long reliance of the city upon the people who work the sea, the city erected a bronze statue of a kneeling lobsterman removing lobsters from his traps in the Old Port, the oldest part of the city. When I stood once more before the Lobsterman, for the first time in a decade, I overheard the words that a man was speaking to his young son nearby: "…and he watches over the lobstermen, and the fishermen, and everyone in the city of Portland. Look, you just put some coins in his hand here, and make a wish, and the Lobsterman will grant it to you." I smiled, pleased to see that the cult continued. Although not intended as an object of ritual and worship, the Lobsterman has become just that. Somehow, even in this modern Christian/secular age, the Lobsterman has become something of a local deity. It had been for as long as I have known it.

I first came to Portland in 1989. I was not yet any kind of pagan or heathen, but had some inclination in that direction. I got involved in a movie club at the Nickelodeon, where we gathered after hours to screen obscure cult films and talk about them from an artistic and philosophical perspective. The guy who introduced me to the club was my best friend, a college classmate who was taking me around Portland and introducing me to the city. Each night the club met, we passed the statue of the Lobsterman. One night my friend stopped in front of the statue, put some coins in one of its hands, bowed his head, and whispered something quickly. When I asked him what he was doing, he said that this statue was supposed to be the spirit of the city, and that if you made offerings to it then it would sometimes do favors for you. A friend of his had been hospitalized with a neck injury, so he wanted to stop and say a prayer for his speedy recovery. He laughed about it, like it was a silly little superstition, and perhaps that was all it was to him. However, he did take the time and sacrifice the money to do it.

Over the years I noticed that my little circle of friends was not the only group to do this. As mentioned above, Portland is a fishing city. If you walk the streets of the Old Port around dawn you will see fishermen emerging from their homes and making their way down to the docks. I spent more than one dawn out at that hour, and noticed that many of the working fishermen stopped at the statue. Some would leave coins, some would leave coffee. When I talked to some of these fishermen they said that it was an old custom, for luck, because the Lobsterman was supposed to look after the local fishing crews. This tradition spread beyond these groups, and came to be known by the larger population as well. Indeed, I am even aware of at least one Englishman who makes offerings to the Lobsterman when flying in to the Portland airport, for a safe journey.

The hipster movie geeks that I hung out with in the club were just the kind of people to do this sort of thing. It makes sense that fishermen would also, for fishermen tend to be very superstitious. Fishing is, after all, a dangerous occupation performed in a terrifying environment. This was more than just a quirky local superstition, though. Some people took the idea of the Lobsterman as some sort of *genius loci* very seriously.

During the early to mid nineties, I got involved in polytheistic religion, first through Wicca and later through Asatru. I started meeting other local polytheists, and sometimes joining them for various rituals. Each of these groups had different beliefs and practices, but most of them either opened or closed every ritual with prayers, toasts, or other offerings to various gods and spirits. Many of these groups specifically had a place in these rites for honoring local spirits, and the Lobsterman appeared in the prayers of many pagans and heathens. One prayer I heard was "Hail Pamola, hail the Puckwudgies, hail Saco Dis, and hail to the Lobsterman." Pamola is an ancient deity worshiped by First Nations tribes in the area. The Saco is the major local river, so of course it has a dis that should be prayed to. The Puckwudgies are spirits that local folklore speaks of, something like elves, goblins, or trolls. Hearing the name of the Lobsterman placed alongside such serious deities showed me that the rites of the Lobsterman had evolved past being a mere local superstition or hipster joke. The Lobsterman had become a genuine local deity to whom serious cult was paid.

This kind of local cult is not generally a part of most modern polytheistic religions in America. Modern American polytheistic faiths tend to focus on major pantheonic deities. However, ancient religions took the idea of local deities with local cults very seriously. Saint Martin is recorded to have found a whole village of heathen people who were willing to convert to Christianity. They allowed him to destroy their temple to the major heathen gods. However, when he tried to take an axe to a tree that stood nearby, that was sacred to the alfs. In other words, the local land spirits were more important to these ancient heathens, religiously, than the major pantheonic gods were. The Lay of Helgi Hjorvarthsson describes how Atli came to worship a bird who gave him counsel. No other person worshipped this bird, just Atli.

 Benjamin Thorpe, nineteenth century Anglo-Saxon scholar, records similar activities on the folk level in his *Northern Mythology*. He discusses the story of an old farmer who had a personal religion centered around a single dwarf spirit who was supposed to live on or under his farm. In exchange for giving the dwarf regular offerings, the dwarf was supposed to make his fields fertile. He also describes a town in Germany where the residents worshipped the king of the local dwarfs, who lived under a great rock at the border of the town. These observations suggest that local cults have always played a large role in traditional European polytheism. Large enough that they may often have overshadowed the cults of the major deities.

 This may seem strange to some people, but that is just because the ancient heathen concept of a god was not really much like the modern concept of one. The modern definition is heavily influenced by the Christian concept of divinity, which defines it as something like "the largest and most powerful spiritual entity conceivable." To the ancient heathens, "god" was more of a job description than a special class of being. Any spirit could be a god. They usually came from certain tribes of spirit beings, such as the Aesir and Vanir, but they could come from anywhere. A single dwarf or alf could be one. A valkyrie could be worshipped as a personal deity. A dead ancestor might be revered as a deity by his or her descendants. Sure, spirits like the Aesir might have been seen to have more power, but they also had more concerns. Odin might be *the* god of war, for example, but as such, he has a lot of things demanding his attention. Praying to him might not work out well, as his own designs might favor the other side. While personal or local deities might not have the great power of the other gods, they paid more attention. A personal god would always favor their person. A local god would always favor his or her own people. It kind of evened the playing field.

 It should not be surprising that local cults like these crop up again and again. There are a lot of ways in which such cults can get started. As the Lobsterman was meant to represent the spirit of the city in a metaphorical sense, it did not take much of a leap for people to pay attention to it as the spirit of the city in a more literal sense. Because it meant something, symbolically, to the fishermen of the city, they were more likely to incorporate it into their ritual superstitions. Unusual Personal Gnoses can create the stories that become the seeds of later myths. Although local deities and their small-scale cults are rarely found in books on paganism, they are found throughout pagan practice. The Lobsterman is a good example of the spontaneous formation of a modern local cult, but it is far from the only one. It is not even the only one in the city of Portland.

To the left of the Lobsterman, resting on the ground, is a giant antique mask of Bacchus, the Roman god of wine and theater. The Nickelodeon was apparently built near the site of a much older theater, and construction unearthed the Bacchus mask. It was left where it was dug up as a historical marker, and to this day local pagans come and pour wine out at the mask's base. At the very edge of the Old Port stands a statue called Our Lady Victory, of an armed and armored woman, honoring all the natives of Portland who died in war. Many heathens leave offerings for the local dead and for the valkyries at this statue. On the other side of the city sits a statue of the poet Longfellow, a native son of Portland. Every winter, local residents put a hat and scarf on him to keep him warm. Every Christmas they leave fully wrapped presents for him. Some local pagans include Longfellow in their prayers, as a kind of patron saint of Portland. I have observed similar things happening in other cities, with other local statues and even exceptionally large or unusual trees.

Over the years that I lived in Portland I came to leave many offerings for the Lobsterman. I have raised a horn to him on many occasions. I have done so with other local deities on other occasions, as well. I pay homage to a number of personal deities as well. Because of this, my particular form of heathenry is not a lot like other forms of heathenry. And nothing could be more heathen than that.

> Wayland Skallagrimsson has been involved in Northern Tradition religion for decades, and is the author of several books on the subject, including *Heathenry: A Study of Asatru in the Modern World* and *New Edda*. An Odinist, Tribalist, and Adaptive Reconstructionist, he believes in taking the best elements of the old religion and adapting them in a way that makes sense for the modern world but keeps the spirit and principles of the ancient one. His website is www.uppsalaonline.com.

Religions of Relation:
Place, Hospitality, and Regional Cultus in Modern Polytheist Religion and Practice

THEANOS THRAX

This article examines three of the core requisite qualities in the consideration of *regional cultus* in modern polytheist religious practice, theological development, and community organizing. The intent is to provide the reader with an understanding of what these three foundational concepts are – "relationship," "place," and "hospitality" – and how they intersect with one another in moving toward realized *regional cultus* in religious practice and approach. While each of these and related ideas are commonly named or otherwise brought up in discussions, both in colloquial usage and in terms of specialized frameworks within the study of religion, very little attempt is commonly made to ensure that those using (and reading) these terms are actually exploring their associative meanings in a critically full fashion. The conclusion brings these three elements together to a clear set of statements of the essentiality of their integration in creating the necessary platforms for developing polytheist religious practices and dialogs which will ensure their legacy of continuity into the future of this, and later, centuries.

Introduction

It is easy to say the things that people want to hear, and to give the people what they want to see: drama, sexy conflict, rivalries and fists rising up against even bigger fists crushing down upon so many, and whispers of screaming revolution and grand change. It is harder, though, to present people with what is *needed*, because often we – the people – are not entirely sure what it is that is needed, and so we buy into one idea over another, at least for a time, in order to sate that rising fear and tension of hesitation that sits on the thresholds of uncertainty. We invest soulfully in ideas which make us feel as though we are part of something that we are able to convince ourselves is better than some *other* something, and all the while we talk in circle-jerk collectives about how our brand of change is different than that other kind across the street. It is harder to present people with a thing that isn't about making them feel better about themselves, or sexier, or more confident. Religion is not about your feelings or your confidence or that glean of charismatic madness that can lead an *army* of us across whatever street of the week it is trending to cross. Religion is about devotion, not only to the blessed and mighty gods but also to the complex relationships that we as mortals hold to this world, to one another as shared or distant or even opposing communities, and to the spirits of the places that we call home, or pass through as wicked strangers.

Devotion is complicated, and in our secularized and politically polarized and tragically globalized world, digitally and *incoherently* connected at a level that nobody could ever have dreamed, devotion is not a popular thing to talk about. It doesn't get you interviewed, or phone-calls for reality television spots, it doesn't get you book deals, or donations, or boards and hordes of volunteers to support the good work – unless you're on that *other* side of the street, with the missionary culture-murderers, but they're selling something that is altogether different than devotion – and at the end of the day is not a thing that pays bills, or bring about fame and popularity, *because devotion is not about you*. It is not about magic, or about spells and power or esoteric hacks for adding inches to your *ego*, but about ushering in a paradigmic shift in which *you are not the spotlit center-staged star*, but a humble servant to a host of holy *relations*.

And yet devotion is full of rich blessings, of the sort that we all love to think we're interested in, for in the candled light of devotion one can discover glimpses of who they really are, rather than who they have chosen to paint themselves to be in their own "heroic" comic book series, championing some thing or another and looking oh-so-good in a sharp get-up with just the right colors and shapes to draw the attentions of others away from the things they don't want them to see. Clever costumes aside, we are all born naked and glistening in some garish light, and if we're lucky we'll die that way too. Ushered back through the katabastic caves of the dark and less knowable, we are not defined by the trappings or facades of heroism and hope that we pin to our shirts, but rather it is our relationships to this world, and to each other, and to the spirits who surround us all from their places of residence within *all of the spaces* in this sacred creation, and to the gods above and below and betwixt and between, which define us in the blooded language of destiny and will.

Polytheist religion is not about *us*, but about relationships *between* us and the gods and the spirits of the places that we enact our great rites and blunderous follies, for a well-lived life will have both in due portions. These are not avenues of identified connections meant to flatter and swell, but to emphasize instead the interrelated state of associated and yet uniquely differentiated *beings*, of which we are but one small and fragile type. We are none of us alone in this or any other world, and are each of us seated or standing in grand arrangement of assorted relations, receiving untold gestures of hospitality each moment of each and every day. Our religions are therefore the vessels and sacred containers by which we *reciprocate* these bountiful gifts, by attending appropriately and in actively affirmed dedication to the accounted-for relations which define everything we could ever know or hope to be a part of.

Religious traditions, both formal and informal, have been developing in various configurations based upon agreements with spirits and gods of specific places throughout the many lands of this world since the earliest days of humankind's walk across its surface, huddled around hand-sparked fires to share the reverently orated stories of the divine figures who first transmitted these ways of lighted, burning warmth. It is easy to imagine, in the light of these first fires, the ancestors of us all coming together and learning about the relationships that were held between all things, and the state of being in connection to the unseen: for these applied relationships brought food to family, and next came the songs of praise offered out to those divinities who were holy teachers and blessed guides.

Philosophies and literary scholars like to discuss the similarities and shared qualities of gods, religious structures and "*meta*-myths" which they suggest guided all of these early traditions. However, each of these erroneously seeks to steal away into reductive abstraction the focus of relationships to specific places, and to specific gods and spirits, with specific groups and people, which is an easy mistake to fall into when one has the theistic removal of a secular-humanist view of the universe. But religions – understood, again, as the vehicles for reciprocated hospitable relations with the seen and unseen beings and forces in creation – distinguish readily these beings, states, and practical progressions from one another.

In the religions found in the ancient Greek world, regional traditions often attributed place-specific epithets to the gods that they worshipped or petitioned in times of need, and great import was placed in consulting with the oracles and diviners that the *proper* form of a given deity was awarded the proper sacrifices, appropriate to the need at hand: petitioning "the wrong Zeus" in ignorance of these regional dynamics, for example, could bring ills instead of gifts. In the living Yoruba *orisa* religions of West Africa, the pantheons of holy divinities have firm relationships and associations not only with general regions but with specific features within them, such as sacred rivers. Though these powerful deities might be worshipped and petitioned a great distance from those places, their relationships to them are not mitigated to mere abstraction, even when they carry a broader elemental context.

Religions are about complex relationships, which exist between the people who practice them, the gods and spirits who are the participant recipients of those practices, and the places through which these all find themselves enacted. This model, presented, is called "regional cultus," for it tethers the identity of the religion – the specific cult structure – to not only the people and the gods, but also to the place and setting which provide the essential context and hospitality to the relationship itself.

In modern polytheist religion, our gods often come to us in vessels of *reconstituted* religious tradition, actively rebuilt and restored after long periods of interruption as a result of genocides and coerced conversions in centuries past, and amongst the most difficult of concepts for the 21st century practitioner to understand is this regionally-specific relationship to *place*, which is amongst the lasting symptoms of the evils of colonialism: the disenchantment of the world and displacement of roots *to the places of the world*, has left us with a world population dissociated from itself. The radical act of polytheist religion's development of the restored devotional regional cults is an act of awakening the deadened nerves of relation to the system states of being through which the holy and the miraculous and the magical *flow through into our world*.

It is easy to say the things that people want to hear, and to give the people what they want to see; it is harder, though, to present people with what is *needed*. However, in this uncertain age, we must invest soulfully in ideas which reconnect us to this world of uncountable relations, seen and unseen forces and beings and agents, of spirits and of many gods, else these ways of true and boldly embodied relation be lost not only to us but to untold generations who will follow. I do not believe that polytheist *regional cultus* is a sub-type of religion, but rather is a core synonym with "religion" itself. Other forms of religious expression are sub-types needing explanatory qualifiers; polytheist regional cultus is and must be understood to be the cornerstone of religion. It is our fully realized relationships, and the dynamics of hospitable regard for those who host us and to whom we must greet worshipfully as divine guests in the places of our life, which will see our stumbling age forward to steady and grounded footing in the place we call *tomorrow*.

I – On Relationship

In polytheist and animist understandings of the world, all things exist in complex relationships, which are visibly reflected and found in congruent form in physical nature, sciences, and social theory. "Relationship" is a term herein used to define the state of associated connection between two or more things, in any number of organizational sequences and arranged agreements, and very specifically does *not* relate only to human-centered dynamics or anthropomorphized configurations. All things exist in relationship to other things: atoms and elements, animals and ecosystems, humans and gods, marketplaces and weather systems. Within an animist framework – which I believe to be essential in at least basic premise to the understanding and navigation of a full polytheist platform of religious engagement – all things in this (and other) worlds are regarded as possessing of a spirit and a "sense of being" in one way or another, from rocks and trees to places and dead people, to gods and thunderstorms. We all of us exist in a complicated web of relationality with a countless sum of *many other things*. (Poly- means many, after all!)

A lot of people who are coming into polytheist religions from a dominant parent-culture paradigm of staunch monotheism or secular atheisms struggle at understanding these complex relationship factors. Understanding polytheist religions as systems of relationships, first and foremost, is an important thing; and, again, relationships wherein humans are not at the center (although for obvious reasons, we take a central role in the active execution of our own practices, being the ones developing those practices). Dualist, monist,[1] or atheo-secularist paradigms carry over into many newcomers to polytheism, who struggle with the number of gods, spirits, or connections, as if they need to "know" them all, in order to "get it" or "do it."

Relationships do not need to be completely "known" or "understood," but merely acknowledged. It is not about "mapping and cataloging" all of the complexities, but instead *having space* for those complexities, and working to develop a lived awareness around our own part within them. For most people embracing polytheist religion in the 21st century Western world, there is a very real need to develop, restore, or *reconstitute* a lived and embodied understanding of – rather than merely an intellectual nod-along with – the requisite paradigms of the acknowledged and affirmed reality of many gods, spirits, and a universe which exists outside the confines of desperately-clung-to human-centered structures of belief and engagement.

There is a tactile responsiveness that comes from the reconstitution of these polytheist and animist paradigms, like learning to drive a car or ride a bike: reading and hearing about it is useful up to a point, but in getting on the road, you suddenly realize that you can *feel the road* beneath your feet, and that split-second learned responses to things like moisture on the asphalt, fog in the air or gusts of wind strong enough to put a little bit of tail-spin into your trajectory are all examples of "things you need to learn on the ground, not in a book." These "tactile responses" which highlight the *relationship* between the driver and the road through the intermediary tires-and-brakes are not often discussed or understood from a place of intellectual knowing or understanding. Yet, we who drive or ride bicycles or unicycles or go-karts or ride atop horses or camels or polar bears, use them every day in our navigation of this world. To operate any of these without a physical responsiveness to the relationships we hold to the world around us would mean, at the very least, a staggeringly impacted decline in operational efficiency and safety.

---

[1] Monism is not itself in contest or requisite disagreement with polytheist paradigm, however certain popularized views of substance monism found in post-monotheist theologies and magickal philosophies which affirm the "one-ness" or "same-ness" of "all" indeed find themselves at odds with polytheism. These in fact decay the very foundations upon which relationship must be understood: the association of differentiated "things."

The Western world has done remarkable things with learning, education, and cultivating the intellect in the last five hundred years or so, and yet has also done a great deal of insidiously terrible things with the same. One such byproduct that does not serve us is what I refer to as *"intellectual entitlement"*: the idea that we have the *right* to know or understand a thing, in order for that thing to matter or hold value on its own. This topic is seen across a wide range of diversity issues[2] in social justice, human rights, and active civic engagement or reform.

For example, many cis-gendered[3] individuals who struggle with not understanding the complexities of gender-variance are made uncomfortable by the request to use certain pronouns to refer to individuals, whose identities and pronoun preferences they do not understand. In the face of lack of understanding, (generally considered "ignorance"), many people feel that it is their right to "resolve" their ignorance by questioning – interrogating and scrutinizing – the people who represent to them a disturbance to their own comfort, (e.g. state of understanding[4]). They fail to recognize that their own

---

[2] Diversity issues and topics relevant to social justice, oppression, and erasure are often brought up in conjunction with polytheism. Part of this is because a huge number of modern polytheists come from under-represented, misunderstood, oppressed, suppressed, or prejudiced communities and demographics. Indeed, the last few years have proven for us again and again that to identify as a polytheist religionist at all is to open oneself up to direct attempts at erasure from many directions, for many reasons, and to face many forms of attack. For many polytheists, awareness and active engagement around a selection of social justice issues is as much a part of their religious identity as direct devotions and offerings, for often it is our very gods who draw us to these causes, or indeed shelter and heal and guide us through our own painful experiences of bigotry, physical violence, and unchecked vitriol from lashing trolls and hate-mongers, as well as neighbors, friends or family that we had previously placed our trust in.

[3] Cis-gender is a term used to describe related types of gender identity where individuals' experiences of their own gender match the sex they were assigned at birth. This term is employed in modern discussions of gender and gender identity, where previously held terms like "normal" or "regular" are understood to be both discriminatingly offensive and expressions of normative oppression, as well as gender privilege. A lot of very good information is available on the internet to understand this term, its usefulness, and history. Gender-variance is a term used here to refer to any person whose gender identity does not conform to the dominant gender expectations of their society (including trans* persons, intersexed persons, gender-queer, gender-fluid, meta-gendered, et al).

[4] A chronic issue that accompanies "intellectual entitlement" is that, for many people, the desire to "understand" a thing is not a desire to honor it but instead to feel some level of control or ownership over it. Where once we may have named things in order to organize our thoughts and feelings and relations to them, the post-industrial world

understandings, or ignorances, are completely irrelevant to the question of that person's rights to respect and identity establishment, and do not in any way entitle them to an explanation, (e.g. socially coerced justification of autonomous value), in order to be expected to render due respect to the persons in question. This *intellectual entitlement* carries over into -theistic avenues as often as it does issues of gender, race, and sexual orientation, and for individuals venturing into polytheism from a cultural background of atheism or monotheism – or in general 21st century Western secularism – these patterns can indeed become quite pervasive and disruptive, and even self-applied. In the context of religious identity, this can cause a person to feel entitled to dismiss the religious experiences and paradigms from outside of the limited scope supplied to them by their society, which poses obstacles not only for learning about how to respect others, but also how to respect and process one's own experiences should they begin to develop into a direction not otherwise satisfied by the dominant culture's supplied conformist methodologies.

The Western world has taught that a thing only has value if we can feel adequately justified or convinced of its value based upon the field of our own onboard value systems or rigid critical faculties, regardless of how (un)developed, (un)skillful or (ir)relevantly informed these things may indeed be. This rigidity, rather than an elastic sense of responsive awareness, gets us in trouble; it gets us in trouble interpersonally and culturally when interfacing with elements from outside of what we feel has justified value, it gets us in trouble when dealing with intellectual concepts that bring discomfort due to a perception that they may threaten our own stances or values (a byproduct of industrial capitalism's "scarcity model" of human process!), and it gets us in trouble indeed when considering or engaging with religious and spiritual relationships or considerations from outside of a reductionist rigidity.

Polytheism is about relationships. Relationships must be understood in an adaptive fashion, with space left in our own "equations of understanding" for variables that we may never be able to "solve" or "know." Our inability to "solve X" does not mean that "X" has no value; quite the opposite, in fact, as any middle school algebra student should attest. (Algebra, in this context, should be understood not as a system of *solving-all-the-things* but instead as a tool for *ordering, organizing, and understanding the place for symbols, variables, and values*, not

---

has taught us that by assigning a name or categorical place within our scope of understanding to a thing, we in fact gain some level of power over it: that this is a complete fallacy is irrelevant, for it is still the *unconscious* motive that drives a disturbing amount of interactions and considerations in our post-modern world. It is this that drives the sense of entitlement to assess a thing's value or force it to justify itself, in order to be considered in any consequential way: things that do not pass this insecurity and scarcity derived control-oriented "sniff test" are at best attacked with hostility and rejection or at worst tragically dismissed altogether, as if invisible.

all of which will be fully and summarily known, understood, or "solved.") Religious algebra, therefore, is a metaphoric tool for *ordering, organizing, and understanding the place for* religious and spiritual relationships, including un-solved variables and known values alike. Relationships, it turns out, are rarely – even in the mundane human sense – displayed as raw and totally understood numeric values, and far more often are variables that we must juggle around in the equations of life as we turn the pages of the lesson plans, recipes, or interpreted ecstatic transmissions that come our way.

Not all relationships in polytheist religious devotions or practice will be direct and transcendent or descendant or two-way-communicative. Not everyone has to be able to talk to the spirits and have them talk back, or use their well-polished "*god-phone*"[5] to dial up every pantheon in the phonebook, or to even have access to this (proverbial, non-literal) phonebook-of-gods. Not every lay person needs to be a mystic, and not every priest needs to be a god-spouse[6], and so on and so forth. It needs to be clear that just as there is an enormous amount of diversity in the gods themselves – because poly- means many! – there is a huge and myriad selection of ways to be in *aware relationship* with them…and with ourselves, and our spirits, and the land around us. Sometimes this relationship is literally *only* factored into practice at the awareness level, as an unsolved and symbolically defined variable, rather than direct and totally understood interaction.

For example, there are neighbors living behind my house whom I have no direct interactions with (by choice, let me tell you!), and yet our yards share a common border and fence between them, with tree-branches connecting them quite literally. If I dug a pit on my property for offerings of the biological and decomposing variety, it would be best to consider my relationship with those neighbors – "indirect" as it is – when finding the correct placement for such, because the overwhelming scent of rotting flesh is amongst the fastest ways to

---

[5] "God-phone" is a colloquial term used in many spirit communities for discussion of various experiences or abilities pertaining to direct communication with the gods or spirits, in either voluntary or involuntary fashions, with a spectrum of clarity ranging from low (e.g. a person with an "unclear signal") to high (which often involves years of training and practices of discipline to achieve). While many do not like the term, it is useful, and has spread so far as to become fairly universally understood in the applicable communities. Not every polytheist has direct communication in this way with their gods or spirits, and that is okay. Having a "god-phone" is not, and should not be, the expected baseline experience: it is generally considered the realm of dedicated specialists, although there are many non-specialists who enjoy regular communion with their gods and spirits in this way.

[6] "God-spouse" is a term for any person who has entered into any one of many different forms of marriage union with a deity, which is a tradition found throughout the world in both ancient and modern religious and spirit traditions.

bring yourself into direct relationship with everyone around you. Relationship awareness gives us the *elasticity of understanding* and factoring variables polynomially[7] into the expressions of our dance through the curtained and dramatic stages of this grand theater of a world that we share with a literal *countless* sum of other actors, agents and elements.

Indeed, this same elasticity must be applied also to our understanding of our own "selves," whose multiplicity of layers and internal relationships must also be accounted for. Self knowledge is incredibly important and powerful, but even more potent is awareness of the spaces that we may never know, the corners we might only glimpse by firelight's dance-cast illumination for the briefest of instances. Discernment calls for an assessment of what is known, indeed, but also to provide intuitively for the spaces that we cannot know to factor in – variables, like "X" – which nevertheless impact the relation dynamic of "self-with-self," and "self-with-world," "self-with-humans," and indeed, "self-with-Gods."

In short, to develop the internal, perceptual, and devotional "muscles" called for in polytheist religion – and any approach to any relationship – you must practice a thing that many other traditions, philosophies, magical approaches and indeed Western parent-cultures have taught us not to do, in word or deed: **get over yourself.** Do this at least enough to proverbially and spiritually and cognitively develop dancing feet and the "elasticity" that allows a drunk to stumble away unhurt from an automotive wreck on the highway, because let's face it: our worlds, and the many, many relationships within them, often lead to collision.

This is *not* a call for lived relativism – another dangerous form of reductionism, valuable when applied correctly[8] but disastrous when misapplied,

---

[7] Polynomial, in mathematics, refers to an expression consisting of variables and coefficients, that involves only the operations of addition, subtraction, multiplication, and non-negative integer exponents. Polynomials appear in a wide variety of areas of mathematics and science. For example, they are used to form polynomial equations, which encode a wide range of problems, from elementary word problems to complicated problems in the sciences; they are used to define polynomial functions, which appear in settings ranging from basic chemistry and physics to economics and social science; they are used in calculus and numerical analysis to approximate other functions. In advanced mathematics, polynomials are used to construct polynomial rings and algebraic varieties, central concepts in algebra and algebraic geometry. (Wikipedia contributors, "Polynomial," Wikipedia, http://en.wikipedia.org/w/index.php?title=Polynomial&oldid=626779316 (accessed September 30, 2014).

[8] "Correctly" applying relativism in this case means, at least in my *totally humble* opinion, a *hypothetical application for the sole purpose of understanding or accounting for something which is outside of otherwise automatic understanding*. Incorrect application of relativism would be the

as it almost always is – but instead for a radically different and critically savvy approach that accounts[9] both for what is known, and for the space for that which is unknown, which allows for the adaptation of that which is known from one shifting state to another as time and relations continue, or indeed the ephemeral unknown coming into sharpening clarity or momentarily fixed and known state. (Also boundaries.[10] Relationships require the successful implementation, establishment, identification, acknowledgment and respect of *boundaries* which reside as defining "things" in the spaces between differentiated elements or agencies participating directly or indirectly in said relationship.)

In shorter? To be "good" at polytheism requires that one become "good" at relationships, as much with yourself as with the wolves and the waterfalls of the worlds, wonders and wights around you.

II – *On Place*

"Place" is a concept that gets talked about a lot in polytheist religious discussions, especially in discussions about regional cultus.[11] In practice, the understanding of "place" should not be an abstract thing, but instead soberingly direct and literal: the location and setting that one is referencing or enacting a thing within. As polytheists and animists it is our duty to recognize that whether in the highlands of some beautiful mountainous region untouched by human shaping or in the streets of a bustling metropolis or standing in the up-draft of warm city air blasting us at a perch atop a towering building of engineered steel and concrete, we are not "*at* a place" or "*upon* a place" but instead are slid glisteningly **inside** of a place.

This language intentionally and by necessity evokes an appropriate amount

---

popular assumption that it means "anything goes! all is equal, all is valid!," which is, objectively speaking, horse-shit.

[9] "Accounts"…as in, accounting, as in accountable, as in literally the responsible *counting and sorting and ordering of things*. The "things" in this case are, as mentioned a depressingly necessary number of times above, *variables* to which we may not have "solved" values to assign. For non-mathematical examples of such critical accounting: in critical debates it is important to account for (or even offer up your own!) counter-arguments to the points you are attempting to argue in favor or defense of, in order to eliminate those awkwardly glaring "holes" in fallacious – that means "wicked fucking wrong" – positions.

[10] Thorough treatment of the topic of relational boundaries is probably beyond the scope of this writing, as it often seems (in 21st century America, anyway… and all of the internet…) that popular understanding of the subject allows for boundaries to only be established by those who do not know how to identify, respect or honor them, while depriving those who *do* of the basic and intrinsic right to do so.

[11] "Regional cultus," being the ultimate destination of this exploratory venture, will be addressed and properly defined further along. Have faith, readers!

of literal intimacy which I feel that most people lose sight and touch and scent of with their casual and dismissive objectification of *where they are*. Disregarding the individual personhood[12] of place is akin to disregarding the personhood of a lover, which – absent a particular type of consent and clearly communicated boundaries for such – would be at best *really shitty* and at worst *actually assaulting*,[13] for it would fail entirely to account for that lover's needs, preferences, no-fly-zones[14] and other unique considerations. As we slide into and out of and up against the various *places* that our lives, religions, and duties bring us, we must acknowledge always the agencied state of those places, for there be gods there, and spirits, for whom it may be not merely home and body and nervous system but also, through their own relationships, the very platforms by which these beings might reach out and touch other beings... such as we mortal humans. (See how it all comes together like that?)

We are all of us in a complex set of *relationships* (see above!) with the *places* that we engage with our religions, with our communities, with our gods, and indeed with our own selves. "Place" refers not only to the physical location (and its affirmed personhood), but to the circumstances of that setting as well; to the specific spirits and deities of that specific place, as well as the physical expressions of that place, and the relationship that is found between that place and other factors (such as calendric flow of time as measured by solar or lunar passes, or the expression of such profoundly important things as *weather* and

---

[12] "Personhood" is a philosophical term that denotes a thing's state of being at a spiritual level as unconditionally warranting consideration and rights, and should not be mistaken to be a form of anthropomorphic or human-centric qualities. Humans are one category of persons, but so are trees, animals, elves, rocks, deities and mountains; places, gods, baby deer and green lichen are all also beings which carry considered personhood, within an animist religious framework, and these may or may not be also attributed a measurable agency. "Other-than-human persons" is a term used in animist dialog to discuss these considerations with clarity. This is the essential concept in *animism*. Graham Harvey's *Animism: Respecting the Living World*, New York: Columbia UP, 2006, is essential reading on the subject of animism, which are to be considered foundational to a polytheist framework. It can take a while to wrap one's mind around when coming from a purely secular and humans-and-animals-as-the-only-things-that-matter-or-feel viewpoint. Discussions of "rights" in an animist sense should not be mistaken to mean "legal rights" in a civic sense.

[13] "Assaulting" is a term that many find confusion with, and disagree about what does or does not constitute assault. For the sake of this discussion, I will clearly state that it is my rigid view that acting in any way upon an agent while absent considered regard for that agent's will or agency (e.g. consent, preference, personhood, etc) is intrinsically an act of assault, or assaulting nature.

[14] "No-Fly-Zones" in this context is a metaphorical stand-in for any boundaries, triggers, taboos or requisite guidelines which all relationships have, whether we have the critical sense of honesty to see and name them or not.

seasonal shift.) Groves of trees, formations of stone and earth, flowing currents of water, the passage of night into day or April showers into May's allergies... these are not mere aesthetic assemblage to assist in the desperate grabbing and reaching after mental balance or sense of inner *meaninglessness*, but instead are – in their vibrantly material presence –the foundations of it all, where belief and practice converge. *Relationship is born of union with place*, for all relationships happen *somewhere*, and that "somewhere" is not merely the stage upon which the actors move but in many ways the most important character in the roll call of it all.

The personhood-of-place, and its hierarchical placement in literal consideration, realized relational configurations and intentional interaction within the dynamics of hospitality and recognized role, are how polytheist religion really *begins*. The places within the natural elemental world are the places where the gods reach through *first* to touch our lives in raw and visceral fashion, and it is these selfsame places that must be guarded not as holiest of relics but as holiest of relations, for they are not objects to be owned but agencies to be cherished, nurtured, and respected. Engaging in actively protecting this world, as a collective whole and in its individual places, is paramount to the authentic and embodied expression of any Polytheist endeavor and identity, for without the humility to know one's place in the natural world one can never hope to hold true piety[15] at the feet of the blessed gods.

Considerations of location are not the only factors denoted in concerns of "place," but also more human-constructed metrics, such as city or national boundary or citizenship (for nearly all religions at some point or another, by force or choice of circumstance, move[16] from a "native" place to a "foreign"

---

[15] Piety, bitches.

[16] The movement of human populations throughout the world, whether because of displacement due to political exile, warfare, economic or trade related migrations, or more naturalistically motivated nomadism, is as old as the human species itself. Archeological evidence suggests that humans have taken various religious practices – evidenced primarily through the remnant ritual tools and burial styles – with them wherever they went, and as they interfaced with different lands, climates, resources and of course culture groups, religious practices evolved. The ecological (place and climate based) influences faced by early religious groups played perhaps the strongest role in shaping the growth and structuring and overall themes of their theologies and cosmological concerns; even at a totally mundane level the earliest and most foundational part of the human religious experience was its localized relationship to place. Movement between different places means different relationships, which means different negotiated structures, dynamics and executions of religious realities. While there are several major categories of religious practice and identity to which the term *diaspora* is popularly applied, any religion which is being practiced in a place away from its indigenous location is by definition diasporic, and whether continuous in its populations' migrations or part of a later restoration of practice will always have

place!), and so again we come to the importance of *relationship*. A person's relationship to a place in the civic or legal or ancestral or nationalistic sense can and will impact *heavily* the way that the spirits of that place *show up*, and as there are spirits in and around and of *all things*, it stands to reason that a person's relational configurations in this regard will impact the practice of religion. Similarly, a spirit or god's relationship to a place may be strengthened by a past or present population's human presence, for our religious and cultural practices can introduce spirits and gods to new lands, just as our movement into and through new lands can introduce these places to our gods, ancestors, and lineages-of-spirit.

Gods tend to show up differently depending on *where* they are showing up. It is tempting and therefore popular today to consider gods in a sort of "placeless" abstraction, as though they are connecting to us only through our minds or hearts, which are ideas I believe popularized by the rise in human-centered consciousness considerations which have so sharply (and I would say destructively) impacted our understanding of theological relations. While certainly our minds supply language and framework and schema for understanding and relating to the gods regardless of where we are, it is erroneously arrogant to assume that *we* are the tone-setting parameter in the equation of divine contact and transmission, rather than the *place* and circumstance by which such contact is established.

To streamline that idea into a slightly different expression, here is a non-religious example of the importance of place and context. If I stand in the shade of a tree on *my own* front yard, shirtless and enjoying the feel of the afternoon wind upon my skin, bottle of enjoyed whiskey in hand, and greet the mail-carrier with a friendly (if distant) wave as he arrives to deliver some parcels, this is a fairly typical mid-Spring scenario. If, however, I establish identical contact with the mail-carrier while standing in the shadows of a tree in *his* front yard in a shirtless state altogether disaffected by the evening chill, whiskey on the one hand and distant wave from the other, *something very different is likely to be inferred*. One of these two circumstances is likely to receive a wave in return, while the other is likely to be greeted by some eventual flashing lights and shiny new bracelets.

A pretty decent metric for initially considering relational exchange with spirits and gods is to ask, "What would it mean if this was an exchange with a mail-carrier (or any other similarly essential civic functionary with whom we are likely to have little or no personal relationship with)?" in terms of establishing one's appropriate *role-assignment* with regard to setting, circumstance, and *place*. Disappointing as it turns out to be for many who have been fed a few decades

---

attributes and qualities reflecting the relationships with both the places that they come from and the places that they exist and unfold inside of in the present.

worth of misunderstood hedonistic ethos, *there are actually rules that govern "stuff,"* whether we care to name and acknowledge them or not. Sometimes those rules are just common-sense role navigation and embodiment (or, in the case of hanging out half-naked in your mail-carrier's front yard at night, drinking whiskey, *transgression*) while other times they are specific agreements, covenants, and expectations held by spirits, deities or entire places with regard to the things that will happen in relation to and with and inside of them.

The idea of rules, structures, boundaries, and systems is probably not what people are interested in hearing about when they tune-in to the topic of gods and ecstatic experience and spiritual fulfillment and trending religious ideas. It turns out, however, that religion is probably not actually about "spiritual fulfillment" (since humans are not the center of it), and that it isn't supposed to be "cool" or "comfortable": those are what hobbies are for. Religion is a rubric for understanding and acting within sacred accordance in relationship with divine powers, immortal intelligences, ancient spirits and local beings linked intrinsically to the very places that we call home, often without bothering to ask how those places feel about us or our presence. These are not concerns for the casual hobbyist, but are of paramount import to the religionist, for it is these structured considerations which mean the difference between right relation and wrong relation, honored relation or one ignorantly transgressed.[17]

Religious structures and systems of meaning and associative context always exist in relationship to the place where they *are*, but may also hold centrally

---

[17] "Transgression" is more or less defined as a thing with violates or goes against a rule, law, or accepted way of things, either literally or thematically. Within a religious context, there are two primary forms of transgressions: *ignorant transgressions* (done either by accident or as a result of a lack of regard or considered care for learning the right ways, or even knowing that there *are* right ways) and *intentional transgressions* (which refer to categories of action, ritual and otherwise, which are intended to transgress those normative bounds and structures for some religious purpose). All religions have *intentional transgressions* wired into them, which are not so much "rules meant to be broken" but rather "actions which are meant to break rules," because sometimes the ecstatic effect of a thing is more important than the structures and rules established in agreement with certain divine powers, specifically because they are transgressions of that established order. They are not therefore "non-transgressive" due to their expected eventual use, but instead, are so important specifically because of their retained transgressive status. Certain types of sacrifice, initiation, rites-of-passage, sexual act, ritual comedy and similar fall within this category, and occupy a special place in religious and ritual consideration. Transgressions of ignorance, however, are a different thing: while obviously more common, they are to be addressed and corrected where possible, and it should be amongst the primary core tenets of religious structuring to secure this process of growth and understanding, that any transgressions present are intentional, and those born only of ignorance are diminished and countered with the piety to develop discipline, learning, and humble growth.

significant relationship to a place where they *are not*, but once were, or will be in the future. While all places are held as sacred, individual cults and traditions may hold *specific* sites and locations as "more sacred," either because of events that happened there (or are held to be events which *will happen* there in the future), or because of relationships between those places (or "formations" within them) and the deific figures and pantheons of the tradition. In these cases, the specific location of the practitioners or central offices of the cult can shape relationships, internal narrative and ritual process in extraordinarily significant ways, for example by requiring annual pilgrimage from a tradition's *current place* to the holy sites and places of their religion, for ritual observances, offerings, or ecstatic retreat.

When there are particular "sacred places" for a religious cult which they are *not* living or practicing in locally or regularly, their presence in other places – either rooted there or nomadically passing through – inherently creates a relationship between their *present locations* (with all the associated local spirits therein!) and the *sacred places* that they in some manner find directive relation with in their devotions. In the big-picture sense of "legacy" traditions which will continue beyond their present practitioners and adherents, *current locations* (even if they are not the "central sacred sites" of the sect) can (and should) become themselves similarly sacred in future expressions, for whatever part those places played in the practice of the religion. For example, a group that travels a "circuit" of seasonal movements through a land – whether due to agricultural and ecological consideration, or due to political relations, or economic ties – may hold the entire "route" to be collectively sacred, as part of a devotional procession which repeats at these intervals.

At no time is a religious practice devoid of relationship to the place where it is being practiced, and rarely are they fully divorced from the places where at least some elements of their origins are initially "from," even if they are newly restored from broken continuity in a new place. These relationships may not be acknowledged by every practitioner or group in the same ways, but the conditions of relationship are not figurative or abstract: the influence and lived dynamics are present just the same. Being on good terms with the spirits of a given place is generally considered to be a good thing.

Not all spirits of all places will respond to all practitioners or petitioners, or even like them, or what they are doing: it is possible to fully and wholly transgress the norms of a place with what you are doing religiously, which can create hostile or even dangerous dynamics. Not all relationships, after all, are good relationships. Some places simply will not respond well to certain types of religious practice, or certain types of deities, or even certain ancestral heritages (at the genetic level) of practitioners: these are complicated, and sometimes painfully challenging, considerations to navigate. Part and parcel with understanding the attribution of personhood of place is respecting its will and agency, which includes the right to not care for you and yours.

As in all relationships, difficulties with the way that a place responds to a certain group or religious tradition might be resolved with the observances of the right actions, in order to bring things into *right relationship* with that given place. It may be useful to find somebody else who has established relationships with that place, to seek suggestions, prescriptions, or warnings that can be offered: it may be that the best thing to do is simply try to find another place, if one's situation allows for it, or else continue to adapt until balanced. In many cases, being respectful of the need to focus on "making it right" and being in a good way with the land and spirits – and doing things like formally introducing them to any foreign gods or spirits who are "brought in with" one's practice – can be all that is needed to move forward toward resolution with these localities.

Other times, however, one's "foreign gods" do not merely get carried to a new place, but instead express newly *through* that place, reaching through the land and in partnered pairing with the local spirits and deities there – through special types of regional syncretism! – and this can be the sort of situation around which entirely new regional cults or traditions are formed. But, first, let us explore another foundational concept, necessary for understanding the successful implementation of regional cultus: the essential qualities of reciprocal divine hospitality.

III – On Hospitality

As polytheists, we practice religions wherein we must respect and in some way (whether through practice alone or direct experienced communion) greet many gods and spirits, that they may be hosted, honored, fed; these are expressions of divine hospitality,[18] which in my estimation makes up the primary function and backbone of what it is to be a polytheist religionist. Forget everything else you've read, or written, or beaten into somebody with a rogue 2x4 on this subject: being a polytheist is about intentionally navigating, embracing, and godsdamned living hospitality with your every breath.

We receive hospitality, whether we want to admit it or not,[19] every time that

---

[18] The Greek word for "guest-friendship" (e.g. hospitality) is xenia (Gr. Ξενία), which is related also to theoxenia (divine hospitality), and these two concepts present cleary the reciprocal relationships within the pursuits of hospitality as they existed in ancient Greek culture. The basic outlines include the requisite offerings from host to guest, and the requisite conduct from guest to host (e.g. try not to be a burdensome moron, if it can be avoided).

[19] And in my experience, most people *do not want* to accept this. I once heard a Pagan in an earth-honoring ritual state, quite defensively, that she held no debt with the spirits of her land or garden, *because she was in control of these things by acting as gardener.* The very suggestion that she held any kind of role (or debt) beyond "master-owner" was met

we step or sit or take a lover to a bed or billiards table anywhere in this world: all things were *created* and *blessed* and are *enspirited* by some forces greater and infinitely more complex and holy (or for that matter infernal and impure) than we. **We are guests here.** And in turn, our religious structures are a form of *reciprocal hospitality*: we provide in our household shrines a space to welcome those (sometimes invisible, sometimes terrifyingly visible) forces, powers, gods, ancestors and holy powers into the center of our homes and lives and families.

There is no more sacred deed in all of human culture than opening one's home and heart to a traveler. Whether that traveler is a beloved family member, a vagrant Thracian priest, or indeed a god of the savage wilds or a spirited queen of the mighty sea winds, there is nothing holier or more profoundly telling of the interrelatedness of the myriad *all*[20] and the pluralistic *everythings* than the warm welcome of properly abided ancient laws of hospitality. Hospitality is, quite literally, the most fundamental and essential *state of movement*[21] within the aforementioned relationships that all beings – be they mortal humans, immortal gods, ancestors, or spirits of place – are a part of in some grand or modest manner.

It isn't about being a perfect host. There is no such thing as a perfect host, for all guests have different expectations. Nor is it about being a perfect guest. There is no such thing as a perfect guest, for all hosts have different expectations. Transgressive infractions, conceived in the sort of human ignorance we all contend with, will happen with each. Some homes require shoes be taken off when you enter, while others will scoff at this or – if they're all wearing boots in the living room – feel slighted or judged by your own removal. Some gods want all of their offered and apportioned gifts to be left

---

with immediate and visceral rejection: clearly demonstrative of a person secure in their dominant position, right?

[20] "Interrelatedness" should not be read as a suggestion of one-ness; for "parts" to be interrelated there is a call for requisite differentiation, by definition and basic, well, math. Sorry, dear readers, for all the math. But the point here is this: many philosophies attempt to suggest, prove, or bully others into accepting, a unifying "one-ness," which is only valid in polytheist discourse and paradigmic explorations if it is correctly applied as a statement pertaining to a shared *substance* rather than a shared *state of being*; our being-ness is differentiated, even if we are made of the same stuff, just as a bottle-opener made from brass is different than a brass .50 firearm cartridge, though they be made of the same material. See? Misguided reductive one-ness is a lie. Unless you *want* to open your ale with a Desert Eagle.

[21] As all things are in constant relationship to one another and to place, and all things have personhood including place, all things are therefore in constant state of many-layered hospitality with all other things. If you're really into one-ness and monistikink philosofetishist reasoning, you could *totally* build a unifying theory around all things upon the basic equational dances of the invariably complex equations of this "meta-hospitality." That would be so hot.

entirely for them, while others want them to be consumed, or dropped into a specific pit in the side of a specific mountain, or left at a specific crossroads, and so forth. Some guests will leave the toilet seat up, some gods will make passes at your sister, some Thracian priests will accidentally make out with the pretty one that keeps serving him whiskeys and beers until he forgets that he is not in the wilds and the caves.

Some hosts will have behavior that offends a guest, and some guests will have behavior that offends a host. The offense is part of the equations of hospitality,[22] which itself is the act of receiving guests, be they blessedly known or entirely unknown and markedly strange in their nature or presentation.

As a guest, I will always inadvertently track the wilds in with me, when I enter your home. I cannot help it. I try to help it, but I always miss something. I bring that which I am everywhere that I go. Sometimes I try to shield the more civilized from myself, but I have learned that it is very much the wildness that they are welcoming into their home in their gestures of offering, of place-by-the-fire, of plate-at-the-table: I cannot be expected to be other than what I am,[23] though as always I will try to affect the role of clean and civilized guest.[24]

---

[22] You could think of the algebraic space for infractions or transgressions of hospitality roles and configurations as the *expected collateral damage* of the collisions we call *life*. I know of no way for any matter or substance or energy to exist absent collision or at the very least abrasive or repelling dynamic, however brief, with other matter, substance or energy. Therefore all-and-everything as differentiated "things" are by their very state of existence in some level of resisted dynamic with all-and-everything-else, which if ideally configured will result in minimal transgression or harm as a result of hospitable relations. But sometimes collisions and collateral. As with martial or mental conflict, the objective is not to ever believe that such collateral damage can be removed altogether, for this would be delusional and would invite blind ignorance to critically essential characteristics and thereby dramatically increase the active harm delivered; instead the objective is to reduce unnecessary collateral damage by following a rubric of measured and gracefully employed consideration of movement through it all, a thing that we call here "hospitality dynamics." Also whiskey.

[23] And it would be a violation of hospitality for a host to demand such, for they would then therefore not be hosting *me*, but a facsimile of me, which would be an objectifying affront to my state of differentiated being. A central element in the purpose of hospitality is to render a clear and observable respect for the personhood and esteemed state of being that the being being awarded such is deserving of; to demand that they be other than they are would be to deny them this respect, and therefore violate them wholly.

[24] And it would be a violation of hospitality for a guest to remain ignorant of the host's normative expectations, and thus a cooperative resolution – e.g. respectful and unburdened reciprocal relationship, called hospitality – is to be achieved between them. A central element in the purpose of hospitality is to render a clear and observable respect for the personhood and esteemed state of being that the being awarding such is

For that is the *flow* of it all: the hosts must endeavor to never make demands or impositions of a guest, though there are always going to be some, and the guests must endeavor to never make imposition or transgression with the hosts, although these are in effect unavoidable. It is not about perfection, but about honor and about considered respect, for the host – who stands as representative of "the place," and from *that* relationship is assigned the role of host – must dually demonstrate respect for those he stands for and those he greets. A guest, meanwhile, never travels alone, for as they receive hospitality themselves they too stand as representative for their gods, for their families, for their lineages, and for the places near or far that they themselves might hold regional dynamic with. No human in this world stands alone, ever: that is amongst the most basic and foundational precepts of polytheist paradigm. It is therefore not about individual perfection, but instead about *intentional, embodied* and *authentically demonstrated* **respect**.

Similarly, when welcoming gods and spirits into your home and shrines and life, you are welcoming them as sacred guests: it is *improper*[25] as a human host to make tremendous demand upon them in the name of domestic decorum. But it is also upon a guest, be they a god or a wandering polytheist, to navigate the norms[26] of the spaces they are welcomed into with a mind for respect.[27] Being a

---

deserving of; to demand that they be other than they are would be to deny them this respect, and therefore violate them wholly.

[25] "Improper" is another unpopular word in modern Pagan thought, but thankfully the Polytheist Movement is here to help restore this basic and vital consideration: things are improper when they are out of alignment with normative structure, and this should not be understood to be a moralizing metric. Dionysian religion, for example, is inherently *improper* in many of its expressions in the greater Hellenic religious dynamic, for it involves within its structures elements transgressive to those of outer normative understanding, which thereby in their basic state of existence affirm those normative structures by contrast.

[26] "Norms" are to be understood as the expected *standards* (which are then also statistically normative *averages*, because I know you were missing the math references). They are commonly understood as the commonly accepted and expected rules or guidelines of a given circumstance, situation, or culture. (Example: it is a norm that you wait in line at an American restaurant, but probably not actually a legal requirement in any state capacity. But if you transgress this unskillfully, you will likely not be served.)

[27] However, as stated above, there is always some level of expected transgression and infraction in this. Not all gods or spirits are going to respect norms of the humans who host them, either because they do not respect those humans, or literally are unfamiliar with the expected norms. This is why many gods and spirits from around the world and throughout the last hundred and fifty thousand or so years have entered into specific normative agreements, relations, or covenants – in the form of lineages, traditions, sects, cults, and the like – to mutually avoid infractions of these reciprocal expectations by having them clearly stated and arranged in understandable fashion.

guest carries as much responsibility, in an entirely different sort of way, as being a host. When hosting the gods, it is important to also remember that we are guests in *their* dominions, travelers through *their* domains of influence, dallying upon the doorsteps of *their* infinities. Act accordingly, as guest or host or hosted guest or guesting host; pour well from the cups of *having* to the cups of *receiving*, and know that someday soon, you may be without home, without table, without fire, without shrine, without walls and doors and curtains, and on that day you will rely upon the cup of another to take in your fill.

The laws of hospitality are timelessly ancient and essential to surviving the modern, and to a certain extent they are elastic enough to stretch into a thousand different contexts, but *always* it is about the relationship between being welcome and being welcomed, and in this age, I find that this is as near to the heart of polytheist religion as can likely be put usefully to word or deed.

Conclusion: On Regional Cultus

Polytheist religion is not about creating "big tent" religious or spiritual bodies or stratifications[28] of big-ticket theocracies,[29] but instead about the promotion of a pious *devotionally*[30] focused intentionality in the navigating of relationships *that we*

---

[28] Social stratifications are the divides within a given group based upon hierarchical distribution of class, wealth, or status. In the anti- authoritarian leanings of many alternative-religious and spiritual groups in the Western world of today, including many Pagan and polytheist seekers, there is sometimes a concern that discussions of organized or structured religious traditions or movements are an attempt to secure-and-abuse power over the many by a few self-selected "masters." This wounded model of power-dynamic is *not* what the Polytheist Movement is, by and large, calling for, in the discussions of hierarchies, structures, leadership, training and traditions which include deferential models of interior relation. Instead, we are discussing traditional models of *respect*, which allow for a *repairing* of so many broken and abused models of power-dynamic, for the purposes of facilitating the restoration of religious traditions, teachings, and avenues of instructing and enriching the lives of those interested in pursuing such. Our world is a pretty broken place, and many of the *foundational qualities of a polytheist paradigm* have been lost to the society at large through centuries of forced conversions and secular conditioning, and so education and modeling of what is meant by (and requisite within) these things is *necessary*.

[29] "Theocracies," e.g. a religious governance at a state or social level, are sometimes mentioned by detractors to polytheist organizational progress as the paranoid fear of "what will come" if polytheist voices are not silenced. I'm pretty sure nobody in the modern polytheist discourses would ever want such a job in the first place, and certainly I am not in any way advocating for such a form of governance, even as I call for *internal* structures of religious authority, for the purposes of restoring and safeguarding our traditions, from the inside.

[30] "Devotions" are central to polytheist practice and paradigm; we pray and worship and praise our gods, and in varying ways have *dedicated* at least some areas of our lives to

already[31] *hold* with the spirits, gods, and *places* in our lives, through measured employment of positive and respectful reciprocal hospitality. To this end, the model that arises – which *must* arise for these ends to be achieved! – is that of distinct *regional cultus*, which acknowledges the complex and differentiated states of the gods and of the people to whom the gods would deign to relate, and indeed the essential quality of the *places* inside of which these relationships unfold. The gods might hold different agreements or roles or enacted agendas or whimsical[32] preferences in different places, with different groups, at different points of our geographic or political world, and as our gods are *at least* as complex as mail-carriers, acknowledging specific context of relationship to them, and to place, is probably a good way to go about things at a foundational level.

"Religion" itself must also be understood in two distinct forms: *formal*[33] and *informal*.[34] Formal religious traditions have an interior hierarchical authority structure of some kind, which governs the actions of the adherents based upon continuity of accepted doctrine, covenant, norms or received precepts. Informal

---

them and the pursuit of serving them, even as we go about our human tasks, duties and functions within this world.

[31] Whether a person acknowledges or practices any affirmed religious relations of any kind or not, they *are* in relationship to places, spirits, and gods, all around them, every day: that's just the way that it is, always has been, and always will be. It stands to reason, then, that figuring out some basic approaches toward evening out their on-board approaches to the world in a respectful manner would be prudent.

[32] Yeah, it turns out that gods often have whimsical personalities. Some of them, anyway. This reality – the fact that they are real beings with whom one can have different forms of real relationships – is something that some people struggle to understand, preferring instead the impersonal and disaffected deities who exist only as symbols of something more-than-us, while allowing humankind to hold comfortably to its masturbatorily fixated self-ideation. Not that there is anything wrong with masturbation, mind...

[33] Formal religious traditions are the more *firmly* organized and structured of the two, and might take the form of specific priesthoods, local cults offering regional ritual services, purifications, or sacrificial observances to the communities around. They may also be entirely insular and focused on private Mysteries, with little or no public (external) "face" or function.

[34] Informal religions traditions are the more *loosely* organized and structured of the two, and are often closely tied to expressions of culture or family practice, sorted according to *household authority*. Some households may take their informal traditions *very seriously*, while still maintaining an informal dynamic: however, a transformation can happen from *informal tradition* to *formal tradition* in certain circumstances, such as to protect traditions and practices from threats of erasure or loss, to secure inter-generational transmission, or to make practices available to those outside of their original group, by way of adopted instructions and transmission styles.

(or "folk"[35]) religious tradition are governed by *consensus or collective authority* which is derived from transmission (and exchange) of *praxis*[36] (practices, behaviors) between groups and individuals, generally with little or no firm hierarchy. Both of these are subject to change and evolve given "cultural climate" shifts, growth, economic circumstance, and relational progressions, especially in the cases of regional dynamics (e.g. geographical moves, nomadism, diaspora, exile, forced/concentration/reservation based relocation), and so neither should be understood as necessarily *static*.

Both *formal* and *informal* religious traditions are valid, and they exist within relationship to one another. In most societies, both are (and must be considered) necessary, or even interdependent upon one another, especially with the rising tides of "New Atheism"[37] in the dominant cultural paradigm of the post-modern Western world, with atheopathic[38] humanist[39] saboteurs finding

---

[35] "Folk traditions" are generally, but not always, of the *informal* variety. In certain contexts "folk tradition" can be very general and refer to all sorts of culture expressions, such as culinary or artistic or musical, and so often *folk religion* is tied very closely to these other culture expressions, in ways that *informal religious structure* might not always be by necessity.

[36] Orthopraxy is a Greek term meaning "right practice," and relates to the practices, actions, behaviors and general conduct of a religious tradition, and is often paired (or contrasted) with orthodoxy ("right belief"). Implicit in both is an understanding of accepted normative metrics for something being "right," by which is meant "proper" and "in accord."

[37] New Atheism is a movement found in Western society and thought today which posits that religious, spiritual, superstitious and magical traditions, thoughts, or practices need to be actively sought out and destroyed, expelled permanently from society. These are in effect neo-fascist ideas which represent legitimate threat of religious and cultural genocides in our world, and while there are open and boldly stated proponents of these platforms of murderous intent, their influence stretches wide into circles that often do not even recognize themselves as paralleling such dangerous philosophies. This is one of the single biggest threats to religion and diverse culture in world history, and frighteningly often dresses itself up in the "soft" language of the progressive-left, borrowing language liberally from social justice circles in a way that suggests it is interested in nurturing and enriching lives of the disadvantaged, while instead seeking to install itself as their new "masters" by way of owning the authorship of their "permitted" thoughts and practices.

[38] Atheopathic is a term I have coined to describe the expressions of atheism and non-theism which intrusively seek to spread themselves by way of competing with – and, as with New Atheism, countering and eradicating – religious (and especially -theistic) thought, belief and practice. There are growing trends of atheopathic sentiment in American Paganism, often presenting as merely secular-leaning, while fighting for a controlling interest in identifying terms such as "polytheism" and "religion," attempting (whether intentionally or not) to gain a dominant position in otherwise religious communities.

their way into even the most mystically inclined of communities. In areas where there is only a folk practice (informal tradition) it may take on a formal identity and structure in contrast with external/foreign structures (e.g. a set of "foreign" informal folk practices in a new land may become formal or gain formal leadership structures, in order to preserve not only the transmission of these practices between generations but also to preserve the cultural identity of the group in question).

Religious traditions of all varieties are to be understood as being born out of agreements, covenants and relationships with other-than-human agencies, intelligences and forces, including but not limited to, ancestors, animal spirits, plant spirits, gods, lesser divinities and deities, elemental forces... all of which are understood to hold a level of affirmed personhood. Religious traditions therefore are the *bodies of belief and practice* which provide the context for conduct, hospitable relation, and regionally differentiated dynamics of deific devotions. They are essential, for just as the mail-carrier's truck and carrier bag allow for the transmission of parceled communications and distributions throughout a vast and global expanse, the fabric and structures of our religious cults provide the delivery system for our devotions, and the dance-steps for the complex choreography found in divine hospitality.

If polytheist religion has a place in the unfolding and uncertain future of our world – which it certainly seems to be preparing itself for, despite hostilities and suppressions from all directions[40] – then it is amongst our most vital and centrally important needs to expand and mature our practical and collective understanding of structured regional cultus in both *formal* and *informal*

---

[39] Humanism is a general descriptor, but also references some specific movements, which in name affirms the centrality of *humans* in the big-picture grand scheme of things, directly, instead of any kind of other-than-human power, deific force, or pantheons of gods and spirits. In modern American Paganism, there is a large contingent of humanism whose presence is found in religions, magical, fraternal and philosophical circles, arguing often against the reality of gods or spirits or supernatural considerations, generally in favor of psychological, archetypal, and "meta-mythological" frameworks inspired by misinterpretations of psychoanalyst Carl Jung and literary mythologist Joseph Campbell.

[40] There are and have long been attempts to silence, control, suppress, redefine, censor and *erase* the words and discussions of polytheist religionists for all kinds of reasons, from all directions, including some who pass themselves off as polytheist themselves by way of appropriated identifying language, in order to subvert the reconstitution, development, and explorations of polytheist religious theologies, practices, and community organization. The reasons are too many to list. May their tongues grow heavy in mouth and their breath turn rank and spoiled as the wicked intents held in tiny hearts.

execution. Within this pursuit will be found the means to secure a place for our devotions, for our relations, for our religions, into which others who will come after us – a legacy of younger polytheists who *will* follow in whatever wake we leave in the name of our blessed gods – can step and securely seed their own spaces for a *reconstituted* respect and reverent regard for the many, *many* gods.

It is a damn fine time to be a polytheist, but more so, it is a damn fine time to prepare this world (and ourselves) for welcoming the proverbial tomorrows, which might otherwise have it in mind to see our religions purged from this world once more. In praise of our gods, let us not lose *tomorrow* before it arrives, by doing what we can *today* with what we have, with what we know, and with what our ancestors (in their brilliant victories or stunning missteps) left to us. In a world lit ablaze with the contrasting hues of advancement and heightened atrocity, poverty, disparity and revolt, change *is coming*. Let us commit to seeing our religions *enlivened* through disciplined individual and interrelated regional cult structures, that we can indeed invest in and endeavor to see these sacred traditions restored in our worlds, newly cast from ancient mold and method in ways that fit into our post-post-modern frameworks of today, with the structures to weather a thousand searing tomorrows.

> A temple priest, shaman, and spirit-worker in the Thracian tradition, Theanos Thrax teaches foundational spiritual principles and results-oriented mysticism, with a focus on anchoring ancient nomadic wisdoms and values in contemporary reality. In all of his doings, he attempts to honor the ancestors, the gods, and his living relations in this world and the rest of them, while focusing also on further understanding and addressing contemporary issues of race, gender, and sexuality.

Ghost Stories of Gaul

MORPHEUS RAVENNA

> Moved by the story of Gaul and the cultural loss that occurred during the period of Roman conquest, this essay describes a few Gaulish Celtic sanctuaries as they might have looked while still in use, before the destruction of public Gaulish religion, based on the historic sanctuaries of Gournay, Mirebeau, Ribemont, Roquepertuse and Entremont. Sanctuaries such as these were in continuous use and development from about the middle of the last millennium BCE until the time of the Gallic wars when they were abandoned and in some cases intentionally destroyed and buried by the Gauls in advance of the Roman conquest. The essay explores an experiential perspective on this dissolution of organized Gaulish religion and its modes of remembrance, transmission and survival within post-conquest Gaul.

I spent a lot of last year poring over archaeological notes on religion in ancient Gaul in the course of research for a book about Celtic war divinities. There is something that moves me deeply in the story of Gaul. It is not simply the religious culture in its own right, as fascinating as that is. It grips me like a spirit; it speaks to me in a voice like the wind crying through a ruin. So much of the texture and cultural depth of Celtic Gaul is obscure: we have a wealth of archaeological remains, and a fair measure of ethnographic information from neighboring cultures; but of their own stories, songs, rituals – of the lived experience of Gaulish life and religion, only fragments remain. During the period of Roman conquest, Gaul was heavily depopulated by war, massacre, and enslavement, and a massive cultural loss and transformation occurred.

I feel that loss keenly. One night, from the dry fragments of archaeological data I was studying while a full moon poured light in my window, a ghost rose up and took hold of me. It asked me to share its tale. This is that story. It contains much that is based on research and evidence, but it also contains much that comes from my own intuitions and received gnosis about what has been lost. It is my offering to the spirit of Gaul, whom I have heard calling out to be remembered.

* * * * * * * *

We are in the soft green landscape of northern Gaul, its wooded hills and valleys crossed by many streams. We are in the territory of the Bellovaci, a strong Belgic tribe. Caesar's legions have not yet come to conquer this land – it is a tribal dominion still. That moon pours light over the landscape, a wide stream that courses by the walls of the *dunum*, the fortified city standing on the slope overlooking the valley. Inside the walls, buildings cluster, their thatched roofs sloping over timber-framed and wattle walls. Just inside the entrance gate of the *dunum*, there is a space set apart from all the rest.

 A tall wooden palisade guards the boundary of this space, enclosing it seven feet high with pole stakes but for an entrance gate facing us at the east. At intervals along these walls stand tall posts, towering over the palisade. On each post hangs a set of battered arms: sword, spear, and the man-sized oval shields of Gaulish tribes, their painted tribal devices weathered and fading, cut and spattered with the traces of battle. Here, a cluster of Roman helms and shields hang, and there, a more exotic-looking set. The captured trophies of rival tribes and nations. Over the eastern entrance in the palisade, a great wooden portal looms high above us. Its double gates are hung on thick timber uprights which support two ranks of heavy lintel beams, as thick as a man's waist. We can see the ornate carvings on the beams and gate glinting in the shifting light. We recognize the style of these carvings: sinuous and twisting, coursing spirals and curved geometries, the artful madness of La Tène Celtic design, brought to life by its colorful paint and the flickering torches to either side of the gate. In the shadowed spaces between the ranked beams of the portal over the gates, we can see rows of skulls: the heads of captured warriors set to watching the gateway between the outer world and the sanctuary within. The gates swing outward.

 We cross a threshold between the uprights of the portal and step onto a narrow wooden footbridge which spans the eight feet of deep boundary ditch inside the palisade. To either side of the footbridge, in the ditch and up against the palisade wall, the skulls of horned cattle are stacked into mounds, all facing us as we move through the crossing. Apotropaic guardians like the dead warriors on the outer walls, their eye hollows watch us. Beyond the stacked cattle heads, we can see the ditch running along the circumference of the enclosure, and in it the layered remains of many offerings: countless animal bones; cattle, pigs, horses, sheep, layered in with thousands of rusted, broken swords, splintered shields, old spearheads, decaying leather scabbards and the detritus of endless bits of old weaponry. For hundreds of years these offerings have been laid down here, one atop another as the older sacrifices sink into the earth at the bottom of the boundary ditch. When the arms displayed on the walls rust and their leather strappings crumble enough to fall, they will be laid into the boundary ditch with the bones of sacrificial animals, and another set will take their place.

In the precise geometric center of the rectangular enclosure, a roofed temple stands, its four ornately carved and decorated corner posts carefully aligned to the cardinal directions. Within its shelter, the hollow altars are delved into the earth: nine circular pits cut deep into the soil in an open circle facing us as we approach from the east; and in the center of the circle, a tenth, larger oval pit. A heavy-hewn table stands before the structure, blood-stained, and nearby also is a sacred hearth and cooking-pits. Here the sacrifices are made to the poetic invocations of the Druidic priests. The presence of their spirits here is vivid to our senses - we can hear the echoes of their intonations, the words uplifted, the beauty of sonorous chantings in the ancient Gaulish tongue. Here the offerings are dedicated – the many bright treasures, the fine weapons, the poured libations. The animals are brought, their blood spilled; parts of their bodies are given to the Gods and offered in the pits of the hollow altars, entrances into the Otherworld. The rest of the meat, sanctified by the touch of the Gods, is brought out and cooked in the cooking-fires, and shared with the gathered people of the tribe. The hollow altars will be covered between ceremonies, and the portions of the animals given to the Gods within them will be left there for the Gods until the flesh has fallen from the bones, and then the bones will be brought out and placed in the boundary ditch, as the ritual cycle continues.

Outside the temple, another, smaller building is enclosed with walls, and within is heaped a wealth of treasure. Golden torcs, arm-bands, necklaces, anklets, belts. Cups and cauldrons in gold and some silver; hand-mirrors, chains, enameled, jeweled, twisting with ornate La Tène ornament. Wooden chests overflow with objects captured, created, offered. Treasures up on treasures, and more weapons – fine, heirloom weapons. Baskets of coin gleam on the floor, some so old that the basket-weavings are disintegrating and the treasures spill onto the earthen floor, where they are slowly sinking in to the soil under the weight of layers up on layers of offerings. Humbler offerings litter the floor, too: ceramic and earthenware cups, fragmented crockery, bronze and iron tools, objects too old to be recognizable. How deep have the layered offerings sunk into the earth inside this treasure-house? It is never guarded except by the spirits. No one would ever think of stealing gifts already belonging to the Otherworld.

In the remaining corner of the sanctuary enclosure, behind the sacrificial temple, there stands a copse of trees. A little piece of the forest that was cleared to build the dunum whose walls surround this sanctuary, this grove of trees was left untouched and simply enclosed by the boundary ditch and palisade. It is a home for the Gods within the sacred precinct of the sanctuary. None but they enter here. Nor do we.

* * * * * * * *

We follow the tracks of ghosts to another rolling valley a little way north. Following the river's tributary upstream and a little to the west, we approach another large sanctuary complex, surrounded by its protective enclosure of ditch, bank, and gated palisade. Its gentle rising hill is occupied by an imposing rectangular temple; its white stone foundations glow in the blue moonlight. The stairs and walkways of its gallery are worn smooth from the footsteps of devotion; we glimpse the spirits of those long-dead Gauls still walking in circumambulation around the temple, whispering prayers or chanting their songs of praise of the Gods who wait within.

Below us, the temple complex cascades down the gentle slope eastward toward the river. We wander past clusters of shrine buildings, toward a corner of the complex surrounded by its own enclosure and boundary ditch. Inside, the ground itself seems to glint with white objects like pale flowers scattered. Drawing near, we begin to discern bones - skeletons and parts of skeletons, dismembered and lying spread along the boundaries. Carrion birds have been here, picking them clean, but remnants still cling to some of the bones. There are no heads to be seen.

A few yards away, a looming structure in the corner of the enclosure glows white by the moon's light and we can see that it too takes its whiteness from the bones of which it is built and the gleaming weapons hung upon it. A square shrine built all of bones it is. Carefully stacked for stability, human long-bones criss-crossed make up its lower tiers; here and there intermixed with the leg-bones of horses. On its outer faces are hung more shields and weapons, and its upper surfaces are protected by a layer of shoulder-blade bones. An opening faces us, again toward the east, and within we can discern a floor carefully tiled with iliac bones, surrounding a round post-hole in which stands a wooden icon with unfathomable staring eyes, its base set into deep, soft layers of human ash within the post-hole.

Here we have found the home for which the skeletons at the boundary are being prepared. As the bodies of the dead are brought to this sacred place, they are dismembered and laid out for excarnation – for the rite of sky burial. Their flesh consecrated in offering to the carrion birds who come as the living embodiments of a dread and holy divinity in bird form, carrying the flesh and spirits of the dead to the sky, leaving the bones for memory. Echoes of distant croaking drift to us, along with the voices of the priests who tend this shrine of death, calling in invocation to the divinity and to the ravens and vultures who know the sound of that familiar call. The satin rustle of wings comes as the priests greet these revered friends, welcoming them to their funerary feast.

When the bones are picked clean of their living remains, they will be prepared by the hands of these priests and carefully layered into the shrine. It is not simply a shrine for the ancestors of the tribe – it is an ossuary built of the very ancestors themselves, thousands and thousands of the bones of the honored dead raised up into a structure for their reverence.

*   *   *   *   *   *   *   *   *

The moon is setting over the sea, its last wash of light cast across the shifting waters in a long evanescent beam. Behind us, the land grows dark. We turn away from the Mediterranean and follow an old track to the north by dim starlight, past ancient villas and along a river, where cliffs rise above the stream. We are in the territory of the Salluvii, southern Gaulish tribes living at the intersection of Celtic and Ligurian tribal regions, and neighbors to the Greek colony of Massilia.

Terraces cut into the stone of the cliff become discernible as our eyes adjust to the low light. We sense presences; beneath our feet, at the foot of the terrace, the skeletons of horses and warriors lie cradled within the land, anchoring their watchful spirits here as guardians of this place. Rising over the terrace, a gallery of carved stone pillars looms over us as we ascend the rock-hewn steps. Statues of seated warriors, larger than life, guard the entrance to the holy shrine, their wide, staring eyes gazing silently beside the forms of horses etched into the pillars. We are in a temple of warriors.

Within the guarded sanctuary, ranks of pillars bearing carved human heads and hollowed niches emerge from the darkness beneath the cliff. If the sanctuary were active, torches might warm it with light, and we could discern vivid painted designs covering the stone, images of horses, carrion birds, and snakes, and scenes of glorious heroic death. We could make out the skulls occupying these niches, shadows flickering in the hollows of their eyes; and we could see how they too have been painted with the same colors and motifs, fusing them into the very pillars of the sanctuary. Dominating the sanctuary, an imposing double portico stands on three great rectangular pillars bearing many skull-niches filled with heads, and supporting massive carved oak lintel beams. Above, a huge carrion bird carved in stone presides over the sanctuary, some mighty winged divinity to whom warriors consecrate their lives and deaths.

Memory resonates here, a palpable presence that seems to whisper from the army of heads. They tell of rites of elevation, of heroization. The heads of the most respected warriors brought back from fields of battle, given the honor that was their due. Of processions of priests and warriors entering the sanctuary carrying these heads, perhaps borne aloft on shields. Of recitations of lineages and deeds, of the chorus of voices chanting the songs of heroes as the heads are anointed, raised up before the great bird divinity, and enshrined into their places. Here warlords and chieftains surely walked and prayed, making their offerings and seeking the guidance and intelligence of the honored heroic dead.

Here youths must have been brought for the rites of initiation to warrior status and introduction to the heroes of their tribe.

* * * * * * * *

What we have seen are dreams of a few Gaulish Celtic sanctuaries as they might have looked while still in use, before the destruction of public Gaulish religion. I've combined elements of a few different sanctuaries within their regions for the sake of illustrating the different kinds of shrines that were in use. Most of what I've described here is based on archaeological records, with elements of ritual filled in from contemporary texts or by cultural parallel with related Iron Age Celtic groups. The temples of northern Gaul portrayed here are based on the historic sanctuaries of Gournay, Mirebeau, and Ribemont;[1] the southern temple near the Mediterranean is based on Roquepertuse and Entremont.[2] Sanctuaries such as these were in continuous use and development from about the middle of the last millennium BCE until the time of the Gallic wars. How do we have such detail about the contents of these sanctuaries? Because the Gauls of some tribes committed a kind of religious suicide before Caesar's onslaught came.

During the conquest period in the middle of the first century BCE, many of the northern Belgic sanctuaries were abruptly closed. The hollow altars were filled in and covered over. The temples were dismantled – their walls collapsed inward to cover their contents.[3] The ossuary shrine made of ancestors' bones was carefully felled outward from the inside, so gently that many of the bones remained locked together in their stacked patterns, and none were broken.[4] Everything was knocked down, including the palisade walls; the banks were leveled to fill in the boundary ditches. And then the entire enclosures were covered over with low mounds of soil. This was not the destruction of war – these sanctuaries were intentionally and carefully dismantled, and all around the same time, mid-century.

At a similar period, the southern temple at Roquepertuse was destroyed by burning.[5] We do not know if this was undertaken by the tribes themselves in a similar act of protective cultural destruction, or whether it was torched by the Romans in the conflict itself or in retribution for some stage of rebellion. Whatever the case, it was burned and brought down to rubble and was not rediscovered until the 19th century.

---

[1] Brunaux 13-22
[2] Koch 1541; Armit 143-149
[3] Brunaux 14
[4] Brunaux 19
[5] Koch 1541

The story unfolds: as the Druidic priesthood of northern Gaul recognized what was facing them in Caesar's conquest, it seems they chose to bury half a millennium of religious tradition literally into the grave rather than see it desecrated by the Roman legions. This desecration was a real threat: Caesar's biographers wrote of how he made himself and the legions rich in Gaul, keeping the loyalty of his troops through massive seizures of treasure, especially gold. That river of gold flowing into Rome came primarily from looted sanctuaries and temples – from the votive treasuries where mountains of valuable offerings were kept for the honor of the Gods. "In Gaul, he rifled the chapels and temples of the gods, which were filled with rich offerings, and demolished cities oftener for the sake of their spoil, than for any ill they had done."[6]

When Caesar came, it seems he never saw these northern temples; they were gone before he arrived. His writings on Gaulish religion describe temples full of votive deposits, as he had apparently seen and looted many of them. But in other places he saw what he described as "constructed mounds" which were venerated, and which he understood to contain buried sacrificial deposits.[7] These, I think, must have been the mounds covering the buried sanctuaries. The grave mounds of Gaulish religion.

I try to imagine what it must have been like to participate in that destruction and burial. Some group of Gaulish people undertook the physical labor of leveling their sacred temples, knocking down the ossuary shrine built of generations of their own ancestors' bones, obliterating five hundred years of memory and tradition and worship, laying them into the dirt as gently as possible and covering it all over, never to be retrieved. And then what… walked away? Went for a well-earned drink? Joined the resistance army with Vercingetorix? Drowned themselves in the river? It's about this point where I tend to give up trying to imagine what it must have been like to do that. But the ghosts of Gaul ask me not to turn away. How does a person go on after overseeing the funeral of their own religion? What next?

Caesar, and other authors of the period, wrote of the willingness of the Gauls to die in battle. It was said that this bravado came from the certainty of rebirth and the conviction that death was not the end, but only "a point in the midst of continuous life."[8] And I think those things were true, but I sense at this period there was something more at work, too. These ghosts whisper to me of a longing to die in battle, not just for the seeking of a hero's death, but also because when one has witnessed the onslaught of conquest and the funeral of

---

[6] Suetonius §LIV
[7] Brunaux 33
[8] Caesar 6:14; Duff 37

one's own culture and religious life, death in battle fighting that enemy may be the only thing left to want.

It is from this period that the springs, caves, lakes, and other natural sites which had always been in use as cult sites, now began to dominate as centers of activity in continental Celtic religion. It is from this period that we see a dramatic increase in votive icons and offerings, inscribed magical tablets, and other religious items appearing in watery sites as the evidence of folk religion.[9] Because, among other factors, after the destruction of the temples and the criminalization of public Druidic religion and its rites, private worship in the hidden places of nature was what the Gauls had left to them.[10] The Gods did not die, and religion continued, now transforming and syncretizing in the new reality of conquest and integration into the Empire.

The Gauls did not forget their lost sanctuaries, though. After the Roman conquest, even following the official prohibition on Druidic religious activity, the northern sanctuaries continued to be kept as sacred ground. While the *dunums* were built up into Roman *oppida* all around them, the grounds on which the sanctuaries stood were kept empty. Now no longer visible even as mounds, with no surviving structures traceable on the ground surface, the people still conspired to pass down a hidden tradition about the sacredness of these sites for centuries after the conquest, protecting the boundaries of the sanctuaries from the encroaching city.[11] At one sanctuary site, this hidden tradition continuously protected the location of the sanctuary for four hundred years. It was not until the fourth century CE that a new temple, now in the Romanized *fanum* style, was built – and when it was, its corner posts were laid precisely onto the invisible footprint of the old Gaulish temple. Writing of this, archaeologist Jean Louis Brunaux said, "the choice of this spot might suggest that throughout the early empire a clandestine cult activity was pursued without leaving any archaeological trace."[12]

I like to imagine how this tradition quietly preserved the memory of the sanctuary, its invisible imprint in the land. There must, I think, have been family groups within which this hidden tradition was passed down from generation to generation. The descendants of the last priests, perhaps, and those who helped them to lay the sanctuary in its earthy grave, who knew the exact location of the buried temple. Somehow this precise, geographically keyed knowledge of the temple's invisible presence was encoded into cultural memory and passed on through the centuries; perhaps by a rite of circumambulation like that once practiced in the temples themselves. I like to imagine the old people of post-

---

[9] Brunaux 41
[10] Suetonius §XXV; Brunaux 41
[11] Brunaux 14
[12] Brunaux 14

conquest Roman Gaul still walking those invisible boundaries, teaching the young the mnemonic keys to their ancestral heritage. Years and centuries rolling by, the old religion transformed and absorbed into a new, Romanized and syncretic one, and still these generations of Gauls quietly held to the sacredness of the heritage that lay beneath them within the land.

This is the story that the ghosts of Gaul asked me to tell you. It is a story of loss and destruction, but it is also a story of memory and survival. It is a story of the ways that memory, culture, and the power of the Gods resist erasure and hold to the sanctity of place, growing silently like a weed beneath the concrete of a dominant culture. It is a story about how the land itself holds the presences and powers of Gods, spirits and ancestors. Nothing is ever truly lost so long as someone remains to listen to the spirits, to walk their footsteps, and to retell their stories.

Works Cited

Armit, Ian. *Headhunting and the Body in Iron Age Europe*. Cambridge: Cambridge University Press, 2012. Print.

Brunaux, Jean-Louis. *The Celtic Gauls: Gods, Rites and Sanctuaries*. Trans. Daphne Nash. London: Seaby, 1988. Print.

Caesar, Julius, translated by W. A. McDevitte and W. S. Bohn. "The Gallic Wars." *The Internet Classics Archive*. N.p., 2009. Web.

Duff, J.D. Lucan: *The Civil War, Books I-X (Pharsalia)*. London: William Heinemann Ltd., 1928. Print.

Koch, John T. *Celtic Culture: A Historical Encyclopedia, Vol. 2*. Santa Barbara: ABC-CLIO, 2005. Print.

Suetonius (C. Suetonius Tranquillus). *The Lives Of The Twelve Caesars, Complete: To Which Are Added, His Lives Of The Grammarians, Rhetoricians, And Poets*. Ed. Alexander Thomson and T. Forester. Project Gutenberg, 2006. Web.

Morpheus Ravenna is a spiritual worker, artist, and writer, residing in the San Francisco Bay area. An initiate of the Anderson Feri tradition of witchcraft, she has studied and practiced devotional polytheism and the magical arts for about twenty years. Her primary spiritual practice is her devotion and dedication to the Morrígan, within the framework of Celtic heroic spirituality. She co-founded the Coru Cathubodua Priesthood, and she is the author of a new book on the Morrígan, *The Book of the Great Queen*, and the Shieldmaiden Blog. Morpheus makes her living as a tattoo artist and she also practices medieval armored combat in the Society for Creative Anachronism. Morpheus can be reached through her website at *bansheearts.com*.

Olympos on the Banks of the Nile

H. JEREMIAH LEWIS

Egypt under the Ptolemies was the melting pot of the Mediterranean, with diverse populations from far-flung parts of the globe meeting, mingling and creating a complex and dynamic culture centuries ahead of its time. Many of the issues polytheist minds struggle with today - how to maintain ancestral traditions in changing times and foreign locales, what is the most respectful way to honor a god from a different culture, why do gods express themselves differently in different places, etc. - were familiar concerns to the ancients. By examining how they worked such things out through their beliefs and practices we are in a better position to create traditions suited to thrive in our 21st century soil.

Setting out to provide a simple but comprehensive historical overview of Greco-Egyptian religion is by no means an easy task. It is complicated by a number of factors, beginning with the fragmentary state of the sources that we have at our disposal for the reconstruction of this religious system. We possess only a tiny fraction of the literature that was produced during the Hellenistic era, and what we do have often consists quite literally of fragments, surviving in trash heaps, broken monuments, the cartonnage of mummy wrappings, or as random quotations in the works of later authors. However, the amount of material that has come down to us is all the more impressive for this fact.

Which brings us to our next problem: the mass of material relevant to Greco-Egyptian religion has not been collected into a single, easily accessible volume for scholars and interested laymen alike to consult. Several very fine collections of primary source materials have been put together, but none of them are what you would call exhaustive treatments of the subject, especially since their concern is usually with the broader intellectual and material culture of Greco-Roman Egypt, of which religion is but one piece of a very complex puzzle. There have also been some excellent academic studies of the topic – the work of P. M. Fraser, Jack Lindsay, Naphtali Lewis, Robert Bagnall, R. A. Hazzard, David Frankfurter, and Susan A. Stephens come immediately to mind – but few non-specialists have the time or resources to track down obscure scholarly journals, where much of the discussion is being carried out, or academic volumes whose costs are so prohibitive that only select university libraries with a decent Classics department bother to carry them. And even then the really important work being done in the field isn't actually available in English. You have to be able to read French, German, Italian and several Scandinavian languages – not to mention Greek, Demotic, and Latin – if you really want to get anywhere in your studies. Knowing that all of this material is out there – material that could profoundly impact your own personal religious practice, but remains just beyond your reach – can be an absolutely maddening experience, let me tell you!

Of course, part of the reason why there is no single, authoritative collection of the material is because new discoveries are constantly being made, discoveries which radically alter our understanding of things. A good example of this was the discovery in 2001 of a nearly complete collection of poems written by Poseidippos of Pella, a Makedonian poet who wrote in the early Hellenistic era and served at the court of Ptolemy Soter and his son Philadelphos. Although a few of his poems had been preserved in Athenaios, the *Greek Anthology*, and papyrus fragments uncovered in the middle of the last century, no one anticipated the range of his poems or the insight that they would give on the life and interests of the early Ptolemaic court. Thus, no one who is at all familiar with the literary remains of Greco-Roman Egypt would presume that our knowledge of its religion approaches anything like completeness.

Another problem which faces the intrepid student of Greco-Egyptian religion is the nature of the religion itself. Although we may today speak of something called "Greco-Egyptian polytheism," it is a bit of a misnomer, for the term implies a degree of cohesion and systemization that frankly did not exist in antiquity. We are conditioned to think of religion as a collection of common beliefs, ritual actions, and supernatural beings which all adherents of that religion more or less agree upon. Admittedly there is always a diversity of views about how the central tenets of that faith may be understood – and these variants can often be quite radical at times: one thinks about the difference between Rick Warren on the one hand and John Shelby Spong on the other, both of whom nominally adhere to a Christian religion. But even this modicum of conformity was absent in Egypt during the Ptolemaic and Roman periods.

Egypt during this time was a truly multicultural society; already during the Middle and New Kingdoms it had become a multi-ethnic civilization as well. Native Egyptians as well as Nubians, Syrians, Arabs, Phoenicians, Greeks, and Persians all lived and worshiped together, each wave of immigrants bringing with it its national gods. Alexander's conquest of Egypt in the 4th century BCE opened up a new wave of immigration and people from all parts of the Greek world and the ancient Near East settled in the land, following dreams of wealth and greater opportunity made possible by the efforts of Ptolemy Soter and his descendents. Although a great many social changes were ushered in by the Hellenistic era, the settlers remained largely conservative in religious matters, at least for the first few generations. Although they embraced their new homeland and actively took part in its political and cultural identity, they also proudly clung to their ties to the old homeland, stubbornly so at times. Thus we often find in inscriptions and on legal documents designations such as: "Nikaia daughter of Amyntas, Makedonian, with her guardian N.N. son of Bizones, a Thrakian of the *epigone*." (*P.Tebt.* 3.815.2) The poet Theokritos had great fun at the expense of settlers who maintained a chauvinistic attitude in his 15th *Idyll*, which depicts a pair of Syracusan women, newly arrived in Alexandria, on their way to attend the festival of Adonis which Queen Arsinoe is putting on for the public. As they walk through the streets they chatter on about banalities, complaining about their husbands, making snide comments about the natives or sharing the latest juicy gossip about the crown. When another spectator asks them to quiet down, they make fun of his accent and pronunciation of certain words since he came from a different part of Greece. (This scene is made even funnier as Theokritos shifts into a clumsy, archaic dialect for the women's parts, a linguistic trick that is often missed in English translations of the poem.)

In addition to language and patronymics, one of the fundamental ways that cultural continuity was preserved was in the maintenance of ancestral cults. Thus Dorian settlers in Egypt continued to worship Apollon Karneios; Makedonians favored the cults of Zeus, Herakles, and Dionysos; Athenians built temples to Athene and the Two Goddesses; and so forth. Nor, of course, were the Greeks the only immigrants in Egypt: Idumaeans worshiped their own "Apollon;" Astarte was honored in the Memphite Serapeion; the Jews honored Yahweh at Alexandria and even built a temple to rival the one in Jerusalem for him at Leontopolis; and the goddess Ereshkigal was invoked frequently in the Greek magical papyri, to name only a handful of prominent foreign deities that found their way into the country.

In the same vein, the traditional Egyptian religion gained a renewed vitality, which it had begun to lose during the Persian period. Their distinctive form of religion helped preserve their separate ethnic identity in the face of overwhelming Hellenization. Especially important in this regard were the cults of sacred animals such as the Apis and Mnevis bulls, the ibises and cats who were mummified in the thousands, the crocodiles of the Faiyum and even in some places fish and insects were given elaborate cultus. The Greeks found this the most curious aspect of Egyptian religion, and remarked on it constantly. However, they were willing to treat it with distant respect (especially considering the awesome antiquity of the religious traditions of the land that they found themselves in) and came to seek an allegorical and philosophical explanation for the veneration of animals. Some of the most respectful treatments of this aspect of traditional Egyptian religion are to be found in Plutarch's *On Isis and Osiris* and Porphyry's *On Abstinence from Animal Food* and *Concerning Images*. Nor was this just an academic interest: many Greeks eventually came to participate directly in the cults of Egypt's godly bulls and crocodiles, a fact that amused the Romans to no end when they arrived upon the scene. The Romans had a much harder time acclimating to this type of worship. They regarded the cult of animals as rankest superstition, and mocked the practice with gleeful disdain, especially early poets such as Juvenal, Horace, and Propertius. Since many of these poets were attached to the circle of Maecenas and engaged in writing propaganda for Augustus' "golden age" after he took Egypt from Kleopatra, the last of the Ptolemaic monarchs, it is entirely possible that a lot of this venomous attack on Egypt's gods is really nothing more than politics translated into the religious sphere. Soon enough "barking Anubis" and hawk-headed Horus were admitted into the Roman pantheon (Lucian even places them on Olympos in his *Zeus the Tragedian*), while the last attested Apis bull is dated to the reign of Emperor Honorius, almost a century after the supposed "triumph" of Christianity. Even Augustus did not disdain to have himself represented making offerings in Egypt's temples, though he is also reported to have rudely commented that he "worshiped gods, not cattle." The Romans were nothing if not pragmatic, and thus willing to look past such things as they understood that *religio* helps keep a populace docile and compliant.

Although religion remained largely an ethnic and cultural concern, neither the Greeks nor the Egyptians were exclusivists in the modern Judeo-Christian sense. They were more than willing to participate in the festivals of their neighbors and offer sacrifices to each other's gods, and in time even this distinction disappeared, so that a Greek might speak of Isis or Sobek as our god (*P. Mich.* 8.473), and an Egyptian serve as a priest of Demeter at a local shrine (*P. Oxy.* 2782).

There were several factors that contributed to this. First, the two groups lived close together, particularly in the Faiyum and the *khora* or Egyptian countryside, where many Greek and Makedonian soldiers and mercenaries were settled by the Ptolemies, granted small land holdings or cleruchies as rewards for their service upon retirement. Living together, they couldn't help but learn the religious customs of their neighbors, particularly when invited to a festal banquet by a friend or when a temple's propaganda spread knowledge of a deity's *arête* or powerful virtue far and wide.

Secondly, many of these Greco-Makedonian settlers took Egyptian wives, since good Greek women were initially scarce in the *khora*. Naturally a husband is going to learn of the gods important to his wife and her people, and together they will honor their household and local divinities, and raise their children to do likewise. The mother is also the one who usually has the greatest impact on the early development of the child and thus it is not surprising to see a strong Egyptianizing tendency among second and third generation Greeks in the *khora*. Although these individuals continued to have a proper Greek education, were enrolled in the *gymnasia* and participated in their city's *boule* and other

> ## A CALL FOR SUBMISSIONS
>
> *ISIS-SESHAT* Magazine Seeks *Your* Content!
>
> THE QUARTERLY JOURNAL OF THE WORLDWIDE FELLOWSHIP OF ISIS (FOI)
>
> Whichever Goddesses, Gods, or Powers you honor, essays on your devotional practices, ritual reflections, hymns, artwork, seasonal meditations and more will be well received in this publishing platform whose readership spans the globe! You needn't be an FOI member to contribute content.
>
> - Summer issue deadline: Friday, July 31
> - All contributors will receive a complimentary print copy of the issue
> - Email Anna Applegate, the executive editor, at hekua.yansa@gmail.com

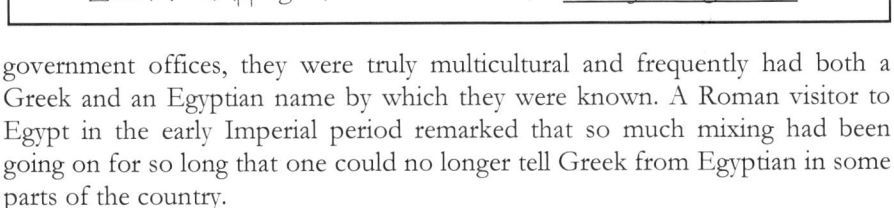

government offices, they were truly multicultural and frequently had both a Greek and an Egyptian name by which they were known. A Roman visitor to Egypt in the early Imperial period remarked that so much mixing had been going on for so long that one could no longer tell Greek from Egyptian in some parts of the country.

And a third factor that contributed to this process was the official policies of the crown. While Ptolemy Soter was still just the *satrap* of Egypt, nominally governing the country in the name of Alexander the Great's son and brother, he met with the High Priest of Ptah in Memphis, which had been Egypt's capital for several centuries at that point. (Ptolemy originally had his royal residence there before moving it to the newly constructed *polis* of Alexandria on the Mediterranean coast, which became the new capital of the country and remained so even under the Romans.) The High Priest of Ptah, who was the closest thing that Egypt had to a "pope" (Dorothy J. Thompson's *Memphis under the Ptolemies* does a great job of discussing the importance of this priesthood, and the intimate relationship it had with the ruling dynasty; there is even some speculation that the unknown grandmother of Kleopatra VII came from this line) informed Ptolemy that anyone who would rule the country must do so as the Pharaoh, and that Egypt's safety, prosperity, and social order depended on the Pharaoh's proper performance of the ancient and ancestral rites. Pharaoh must ensure that the Nile flooded in due season and the only way that this would happen is if Egypt's gods were kept in good spirits through regular gifts to their priests, the construction of elaborate temples, and the great festivals were celebrated in every part of the land. The people of Egypt understood this well and they would not tolerate a ruler who did not perform all of the duties of Pharaoh.

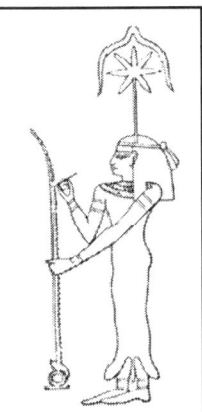

The Persians had failed to heed his predecessor's advice. They despoiled the temples, carrying the treasures away to distant lands. They impoverished the priesthood and abolished the cults of the gods. Blasphemy of all blasphemies, they even slew the sacred Apis bull! (It should, perhaps, be noted that some scholars question the Egyptian account of things, since this seems to fly in the face of the otherwise tolerant religious policy that the Persians employed in governing subject lands. However, considering the abundance of evidence we have concerning this matter, I think it safe to side with the Egyptians and assume more was going on than just a resentment of high taxation.) For such grave impiety, they were punished with destruction at the hands of Alexander the Great, who came like Horus, the Avenger of his Father, to liberate the land of Egypt.

And now Ptolemy, too, could be Horus, who manifested himself in the body of the living Pharaoh, and make things right. And Ptolemy, ever the wise and calculating general, one of Alexander's most trusted advisors, agreed to the demands of the High Priest of Ptah, and from that moment on had himself represented in the guise of the traditional Egyptian Pharaoh. Although Soter could not read the hieroglyphic texts (according to Plutarch in his *Life of Antony*, no Ptolemy could until Kleopatra VII, though some scholars have begun to question this claim) he was advised in his duties by representatives from the various priesthoods and even had an account of Egyptian history and religion written in Greek by Manetho, a native Egyptian priest from Sebennytos, so that he could better understand the mind of his people and the responsibilities that came with the crown. He dutifully performed all of the ceremonies required of him. He conducted an expedition to retrieve the temple treasures from foreign lands, built lavish temples for the Egyptian gods, and made extravagant donations to the priesthood of land and gold won through battle, all of which is recounted in the *Satrap Stele*, which was erected by the Egyptian priests to honor his benefactions early in his reign. Additionally, as Diodoros Sikeliotes relates (1.84.8) he funded the burial of the Apis bull out of his own coffers, at a cost of what would amount to around six and a half million dollars in today's currency. In every way, Ptolemy sought to promote the revival of Egyptian culture, and even elevated native Egyptians to prominent positions at his court.

Needless to say, he was immensely popular with both the Egyptian priesthood and populace, and his descendents were careful to follow in his footsteps, cultivating an image of themselves as traditional-minded Pharaohs with a strong working relationship with the priesthood (especially at Memphis) who ensured the loyalty of the native Egyptians (except at Thebes, which was often a hotbed of dissent and at times even open rebellion, largely because the Thebans were jealous of the prestige of Memphis, which had closer ties to the crown as a result of its more favorable geographic location). As a means of attaining upward mobility, many Greeks at court followed suit, funding festivals

(*IG* 12.7.506), building shrines (*P.Cair. Zen.* 2.59168), and generally participating in Egyptian religion (*OGIS* 89). Even poets such as Theokritos, Kallimakhos, and Apollonios Rhodios incorporated Egyptian mythological material in their writings, as Susan A. Stephens has shown in *Seeing Double: Intercultural Poetics in Ptolemaic Alexandria*, disproving the assertions of previous scholars that the Ptolemaic court represented a secluded oasis of elite Greek culture in the midst of the barbaric hinterlands, with the intellectuals pointedly ignoring the natives and their gods. Thus in many respects the fusion of Greek and Egyptian culture occurred simultaneously from the top down (through court support) and the bottom up (through intermarriage and cohabitation).

But the Ptolemies in Egypt did not turn their backs on their ancestral traditions. Janus-like they presented two faces to the world, one Egyptian the other Greek. They took a direct hand in the promotion of Greek cults, especially those gods who had been important in Makedonia. They claimed direct descent from Zeus, Herakles, and Dionysos (*OGIS* 54), and in some instances claimed to be incarnating the gods themselves (Plutarch, *Life of Antony* 26.1-3). A suburb of Alexandria was named Eleusis and had mysteries of Demeter and Kore imported there (Strabo 17.16). As we saw earlier, Arsinoe oversaw the celebration of mysteries in honor of Adonis and Aphrodite, and the fourth Ptolemy instituted reforms in the worship of Dionysos (*Berlin Papyrus* No. 11774, *verso*). In Alexandria they built the famous Mouseion, which was presided over by a priest of Apollon and the Mousai (Vetruvius, *On Architecture* 7.4). The Mouseion housed the great Library of Alexandria, which was created with the intent to collect all of the world's literature together in one place, Greek and barbarian alike, and was also home to scholars paid by the crown to explore the fields of mathematics, astronomy, physical science, literature, philosophy and the arts. The scholars of the Mouseion made such great strides in all of these fields that one can, without any hint of hyperbole, state that they changed the course of human history. (A good, general introduction to the Mouseion and its intellectual accomplishments can be found in *The Rise and Fall of Alexandria: Birthplace of the Modern World* by Justin Pollard and Howard Reid.) In Greece itself the Ptolemies were greatly active in the promotion of Hellenic culture and religion. They put down tyrannies (Diodoros Sikeliotes 20.100.4) and enacted democratic reforms (the *Itanos Decree*). They funded the reconstruction of temples (Pausanias 1.17.2) and financed priesthoods and massive festivals such as that of Artemis Leukophryene (*Syl3* 557). They had themselves initiated into the mysteries of Samothrake (*IG* 12.8.227) and competed successfully at the Olympics and other Panhellenic festivals (*P.Mil.Vogl.* 13.31-34). In fact, they even founded their own Ptolemaeia festival in honor of Soter, which in time came to rival the prestige of the Olympic and Isthmian Games, with athletes and sacred envoys from all parts of Greece attending (*SEG I* 366). Above all they understood that their power and wealth depended on the favor of the gods, and did their utmost to cultivate that *kharis* or reciprocity.

The final factor that we shall consider in this discussion, which contributed in an important way to the formation of a Greco-Egyptian religiosity, is the concept of syncretism which allowed people to see in their neighbors' gods a reflection of their own. The common view is that syncretism is the equation of deities – that Zeus really is Ammon, simply understood in a different social context. And that makes a certain kind of sense – especially when comparing two deities that overlap extensively and not just in ways that logically follow from their primary attributes, as we see for instance with Osiris and Dionysos or Hathor and Aphrodite, for whom one can come up with hundreds of points of contact – but it's really just one form of syncretism. For the ancient Egyptians, syncretism could be a temporary process: two separate deities temporarily cohabiting together, their essences merging to form a third entity (Apis as the *ba* or soul of Osiris becomes Oser-Apis or Serapis) or a hyphenated double-god (Bawy, who is Seth and Horus the Elder united). Once they had accomplished the task for which this epiphany was necessary, they would split apart again and retain their distinct identities.

In some cases we see the sharing of certain attributes, powers, and character traits among the gods. It is as if one deity was dressing up in the costume of another and acting in the role usually assigned to that other deity. For instance, there are numerous terracotta statues depicting Isis in the posture of Aphrodite, lifting up her skirt to reveal her *pudenda*. In such instances Isis is hailed as the goddess of love, sexuality, and the patron of courtesans, a role not previously given to her. Although these images are usually labeled Isis-Aphrodite, we should understand them as reflecting Isis taking on the *persona* of Aphrodite, and wielding her powers as her own. There is a solid basis for this kind of thing in the lore: in one famous Egyptian story (found in the *Turin Papyrus*) Isis tricked the god Re into revealing his true name to her, whereby she was able to acquire his magical powers for herself. Similarly, in Greek myth Aphrodite gave her golden girdle to Hera so that she could use its erotic power to seduce her husband Zeus in order to distract him during a pivotal moment in the Trojan War (Homer, *Iliad* 14.159;187). However, at no time are the distinct identities of either deity in danger of being conflated.

Although syncretism had existed long before the Greeks came to Egypt (and was a theological expression found among both cultures) the Hellenistic era has often been described as the age of syncretism, *par excellence*. It was the time when major syncretic deities emerged out of the shifting cultural matrix and became powerful, independent figures in their own right. Serapis (who had existed as a minor figure in Egyptian religion from at least the New Kingdom, but experienced a meteoric rise to prominence once he was adopted as the patron deity of Alexandria and given special favor as a dynastic god, the result of the revelatory dream he had given Ptolemy Soter) and Hermes Trismegistos (a fusion of Hermes and Thoth, under whose name a whole body of esoteric magic and Middle Platonic philosophy was written) are perhaps the most famous gods of this era, but there were also deities such as the lion-headed lord of eternity Aion; the rooster-headed, snake-footed Gnostic demiurge Abrasax; Arsinoe-Aphrodite Zephyritis, the protector of sailors and the broken-hearted; and all the assorted syncretic manifestations of Hermes: Hermanubis, Hermekate, Hermathene, Hermaphroditos, Hermares, Hermes-Antinous, Hermapollon, Hermammon, Hermosiris, Hermeros, Hermarpokrates, Hermerakles, and Hermagathosdaimon, etc. (No doubt there were others as well, but these are just the ones that I've been able to track down citations for!)

Although we have examples of syncretism in artwork from the period (the fascinating representations of Horus wearing the armor of a Roman soldier come immediately to mind), as well as the writings of important authors of high literature (both Cicero's *On the gods* and Plutarch's *On Isis and Osiris* deal extensively with the topic) and even on the level of actual cultus – a priestess of Aphrodite who tends the sacred cow of Hathor (*PSI* 4.328) or the dedication to Dionysos which includes an epithet normally reserved for Osiris (*OGIS* 1.130) – the Greek magical papyri (*PGM*) remain one of our clearest and most reliable glimpses at how syncretism actually occurred in antiquity. These random scraps of papyrus and pottery shards upon which spells, formulas, ritual procedures, and magical recipe books were written are a testament to a living and vital faith as it was being experienced by the average man and woman on the street. They are a record of visions and hopes, fears and obsessions, a spirit-haunted, god-filled dream-like world in which all of the old certainties have fallen away, and man is left grappling for something solid, whether that be magical power, communication with the divine, or just someone to love them back. Here, experiences are still white-hot and new; they haven't had time to grow old and solid and respectable in order to become enshrined as part of the traditional, civic or temple-sponsored cultus. Nor have the ideas yet been rendered abstract, systematized and toothless by philosophizing. Here we find it raw, direct, confusing, and messy – but real experiences recorded by real people, and thus worthy of our consideration.

And the picture that emerges from a study of the *PGM* is a fascinating one indeed. We see the Olympian deities not as the beautiful, idealized figures familiar to us from Classical poetry and art, but as powerful, archaic and at times frightening personalities, much more in line with how the early Greeks saw them before they fell under the spell of Homer's sanitizing Muse. In the same text Zeus and Aphrodite may rub shoulders not just with Osiris and Nephthys – which is only to be expected in texts written in Greek but found in the sands of Egypt – but also with the Jewish god and Christian angels and Mesopotamian Ereshkigal and Persian Mithras and a host of shadowy daimones whose names are nothing more than a string of barbaric-sounding syllables. All the old boundaries have collapsed, and the people pray desperately to anyone who will hear them. And yet, we also find old myths and rituals that haven't seen the light of day for a thousand years given a new life, and we wonder how the person scribbling their spell on a piece of papyrus came by this obscure knowledge, suggesting an even stronger continuity of tradition than we have been led to believe existed at this time. Even for those with no interest in the practice of magic, the texts of the *PGM* are an important tool in uncovering the nature of Greco-Egyptian beliefs and practices on the common, folk level.

In a similar way we have a wealth of information on the domestic worship that was carried out by the individual in their home. The small niches that they carved in the wall to house their family's gods, the offerings that they set out for them and regular – sometimes daily – rituals that they performed in their gods' honor, the religious customs attached to family life and civic identity, the wealth of festivals that an individual family or a small community participated in, the records of minor miracles, important dreams, curious visions and strange occurrences that individuals felt the need to tell friends and family about in private letters, or record in monumental stelai for all to see, the votive gifts and major sacrifices that were left at a temple when a god had intervened favorably in one's life, the prayers for healing, fertility, protection, and vengeance which were constant concerns of the people at that time: all of this and so much more has come down to us, providing a record of a living faith, one that is far more individual and direct than we are often led to believe ancient religion was experienced as.

Hopefully, by this point, I have succeeded in accomplishing the task that I set for myself at the start – to give my readers a simple yet comprehensive understanding of what Greco-Egyptian religion was like in antiquity. I think one of the best ways that I have seen it described (in David Frankfurter's *Religion in Roman Egypt: Assimilation and Resistance*) was as a series of concentric but overlapping circles. He went on to describe each of the numerous spheres. There was the individual, the familial, the local, the regional, the national, and the Pan-Mediterranean. Each level had its own concerns, its own way of understanding and speaking about the gods, its own customs and religious practices. Although these levels were distinct from each other – and sometimes brought into conflict as a result – there was also a great deal of commonality and fluidity, and one might draw on different levels at different times to articulate and negotiate one's experiences.

In other words, the Greco-Egyptian tradition was like a grand mosaic, made up of many different pieces with many different textures and colors. What you see when you look at the mosaic depends on where you're standing and what part of the mosaic you are looking at. Step far back and a smooth, beautiful image presents itself to you. Get a little closer and you see the jagged pieces that appear to have been randomly fixed in place, jarring and contradictory and perhaps even a little ugly. Look even closer, at a single pebble or shard of polished stone, and your impression again changes. In the same vein, what we see when we study ancient Greco-Egyptian religion depends on where we're looking, and sometimes what we expect to find when we look there. There is the high culture of the Ptolemaic court with its poets and philosophers heatedly debating this or that obscure Homeric verb, and the peasant woman in her mud-brick hovel bowing to her god in its small niche shrine, the statue black from the soot of incense and the grime of the decades. There is the Roman tourist who has come to see the famed crocodile god of Egypt, and possibly feed it a bit of cheese and bread – after all, this season Egypt is in vogue back home and all his friends have already made the trip – and there is the canny old priest whose job it is to care for the sacred crocodile, who has learned to call him Kronos or one of the Dioskouroi, and not Sobek or even Soknopaios, because it flatters the visitors to let them see their gods in his own, and they are more generous with their coins that way.

Greco-Egyptian religion has a definite feel, a definite spiritual quality to it. It is dream-like, constantly shifting, defying easy categorization. In a word it is fluid – but you can easily recognize it when you see it, even if you can't entirely say why that is. I suppose that is really only appropriate for a religion that grew out of a culture that placed such a great importance upon the Nile river and the Mediterranean Sea.

> Sannion is a mantis ("diviner") and Orpheoteleste ("specialist in Orphic rites") with over two decades' worth of experience worshiping Dionysos and his retinue of gods and spirits. He is a prolific writer and provocateur who publishes under the pseudonym "H. Jeremiah Lewis."

Universality and Locality in Platonic Polytheism

EDWARD P. BUTLER

In a famous quote reported by his biographer Marinus, Proclus says that a philosopher should be like a "priest of the whole world in common." This essay examines what this universality of the philosopher's religious practice entails, first with reference to Marinus' testimony concerning Proclus' own devotional life, and then with respect to the systematic Platonic understanding of divine 'locality'. The result is, first, that the philosopher's 'universality' is at once more humble than it sounds, and more far-reaching; and second, that the meaning of *locality* in the Platonic metaphysics is more flexible and dynamic than we might have expected. Particular attention is given to the relations of 'universality' and 'particularity' as they exist among the Gods, and to the account in Proclus' *Timaeus* commentary concerning the places sacred to the Gods as immaterial intervals (*diastêmata*) not identical to physical places, and the consequences of this for understanding changes in the religious life of places and in the localization of cults.

In his reverential biography of his instructor Proclus, Marinus of Neapolis records a maxim Proclus apparently held to be of the first importance concerning the correct relationship of the philosopher to religion:

> One maxim that this supremely pious [*theosebestatos*] man had always at hand and was always uttering was that it befits the philosopher not to worship [*therapeutên*] in the manner of a single state [*polis*] or according to the hereditary customs of a few [*par'eniois patriôn*], but to be the priest [*hierophantên*] of the whole world in common. (*VP* §19)[1]

The present essay seeks to understand what this religious role of the philosopher meant to Proclus, and what it might mean for polytheists today. Specifically, what relationship does this maxim imply between the philosopher and the many national, regional, or local traditions?

It was clearly not Proclus' intention to impose upon local and national traditions the weight of a substantive universal. Indeed, Marinus himself gives

---

[1] *VP* = Marinus, *Vita Procli*, ed. Boissonade, 1814; English translation in Mark Edwards, *Neoplatonic Saints: The Lives of Plotinus and Proclus by their Students* (Liverpool: Liverpool University Press, 2000), translations freely modified throughout.

us examples of Proclus writing hymns to Gods who are almost defined by their local or regional character: Marnas of Gaza, Asclepius Leontuchos of Ascalon, Theandrites "a God much honored among the Arabs," "Isis who is still honored in Philae" (*VP* §19). Though these hymns do not survive, it would be preposterous to suggest that Proclus worshiped these Gods as abstract, eidetic entities. Proclus, like his instructor Syrianus before him, states clearly that mortals cannot know how many Gods there are, though there cannot be fewer than the classes deriving from an adequate dialectical division of Being.[2] The number of ontic hypostases is sufficiently small, however, and sufficiently determinate, as to make the idea that the number of Gods is unknowable to us ridiculous if that number is supposed to be determined by the divisions of Being. Nor does it make much sense to imagine Proclus writing hymns to deities who were mere local specifications of universal—and conveniently Hellenic—formulae or schemata. Indeed, in the very midst of one of his surviving Hellenic hymns, we find an invocation of the Roman God Janus.[3] In this, Proclus follows the example of Plato, who chooses not to syncretize the Egyptian Gods Thoth and Amun, e.g., as Hermes and Zeus, rather transliterating their names as *Theuth* and *Ammôn* (*Phaedrus* 274c-d). And even in the case of a deity with a long tradition of Hellenic syncretism, namely Kybele, known to Greeks as "the Mother of the Gods" and identified with Rhea, there seems to be an attention to national origin implied in Marinus' remark that Proclus "every month celebrated the rites of the Great Mother [*Mêtrôiakas*], of which the Romans, or rather the Phrygians before them, are devotees," (*VP* §19).

It seems the case, rather, that Proclus put his maxim about the philosopher as a priest of the whole world in common into practice, not through imposing a simplifying eidetics upon the diversity of national, regional, and local cults, but through a most resolute eclecticism. Indeed, when Proclus is critical elsewhere of appeals to national, ethnic or ancestral identity, it is not on behalf of a universal humanity that he speaks, but with regard to the complexity of the factors that bear upon the formation of the individual soul and impart to it a peculiar character and destiny. Hence "nobility of birth according to natural succession" or "the discrimination that has regard to the city-states of our world and the places on the earth" is no more than a cause of "conceit" and "empty arrogance" to souls, whereas "the stable and eternal nobility of birth in souls depends upon the Gods around whom they have been sown, and upon the

---

[2] See my discussion of this issue in "The Gods and Being in Proclus" *Dionysius* 26 (2008), pp. 93-114.
[3] Hymn VI in R. M. van den Berg, *Proclus' Hymns: Essays, Translations, Commentary* (Leiden: Brill, 2001).

divine powers underneath which they have been ranked," (*In Alc.* 112.19-113.13).[4]

Proclus' eclecticism is not that of the dilettante, to be sure; Marinus states that "he was more careful in observing the *dies nefasti* of the Egyptians than they are themselves," (*VP* §19). But he also adds to his practices through "revelation" (*epiphaneia*, ibid., p. 45.5). Revelation and theophany seem to occupy a fundamental place in Proclus' worship, Marinus recounting numerous such moments of personal *gnôsis* in his biography, beginning with Proclus' special relationship with Athena, whom we may regard as his patron, or as Marinus terms her,

> his nurse and midwife, as it were ... the tutelary Goddess of Byzantium, who first became at this time the cause of his being, since he was born in her city, and subsequently took care that he turn out well when he came to boyhood and adolescence. For she, appearing to him in a dream, exhorted him to philosophy. This, I think, is the reason for his strong association with this Goddess, so that he celebrated her festivals particularly and observed her rites with great enthusiasm. (*VP* §6)

Edwards, p. 66 n. 66, argues that either Rhea or Hekate must be intended here, on account of their importance in Byzantium (modern Istanbul), and decides in favor of Rhea, but Berg, p. 307, thinks rather that the passage refers to Athena, with which I am inclined to agree, based upon the subsequent theophany of Athena Marinus records, in which she is styled "the philosopher Goddess" (§30). Proclus' attachment to Athena, having its inception in a certain respect from the place in which he was born, deepens through his choice of profession, but is not a result of his being a philosopher, i.e., does not merely express Her presiding over this profession, any more than it is reducible to his city of birth, but is rather the *cause* of his being a philosopher, through the personal impact upon him of the dream in which she appears, and as the fruition of a maturing devotion. Commentators will tend to treat accounts like this, or the other numinous events and epiphanies in Proclus' life described by Marinus, as 'hagiographical' moments, the significance of which lies primarily in the *objective* sanctity they accord to Proclus' person, but they have significance as well for understanding how Proclus himself approached his religion, his openness to allowing direct experience of the Gods, even unsought, to play a guiding role in his practice. This offers support for the Gods having personal agency for Proclus, as well as the worshiper, neither being reducible to parts in a

---

[4] *Proclus: Commentary on the First Alcibiades*, L.G. Westerink (ed.) & W. O'Neill (trans.) (Westbury, Wiltshire: Prometheus Trust, 2011).

cosmic machine; and this in turn accords with the systematic emphasis in Proclus upon the autarchy of the henads, or Gods, and the irreducibility of the one-on-one encounter between God and worshiper.

The universality of the philosopher's religion as we see it in Proclus' biography is not a mastery *a priori* of every tradition through the possession of a superior, philosophical knowledge, not the essentialist reduction of theophany to eidetics, but rather the philosopher's radical *openness* to every tradition. This openness reflects the metaphysical priority of individual Gods or henads to the pantheon structure, insofar as the latter is a *whole*, and henads transcend the status of being parts of a whole. The *totality* that the philosopher embodies, then, in her cosmopolitanism, is not ontically secured, a totality of essence, but a higher, existential totality of the kind that Damascius speaks of in the early pages of his *De principiis*, a totality which does not *totalize*, and which is in this respect without principle (*anarchos*) and without cause (*anaitios*).[5] What, then, does the philosopher, in this radical openness to individual Gods in their ineffable uniqueness, have to offer the local, regional and national cults who remain within the boundaries of their discrete illuminations? During Proclus' sojourn in Lydia, for example, he is initiated "into the more ancient rites still practiced there," and "acquired clear knowledge [*epegignôske*] of their customs," (*VP* §15) where the verb suggests, not essentializing knowledge (*epistêmê*), but rather acquaintance, witnessing; but with the result that "for their part, if through length of time they [the Lydians] had neglected any of the practices, they learned from the philosopher's directions to serve the Gods more perfectly," (ibid.). What is the nature of this exchange between philosopher and cult?

Marinus gives us a glimpse of Proclus' real-time interaction with a local cult in his account of an episode that occurred during Proclus' sojourn in Lydia:

> Moreover the God in Adratta clearly revealed his affinity with this man who was dear to the Gods. For when Proclus visited his sanctuary he received him graciously with manifestations. Proclus was in perplexity, and prayed to learn what God or Gods frequented the place and were honored there, since different tales prevailed among the locals. Some opined that the temple belonged to Asclepius and had many signs to confirm this ... But others believed that the Dioscuri frequented the place ... For this reason then, as has been said, the philosopher was perplexed, unable to disbelieve the reports; and as he begged the Gods of the place to disclose their identity to him, it seemed to him that the God visited him in a dream and gave him this clear prompting: "What

---

[5] *De principiis*, edd. Westerink & Combès, vol. 1, p. 2.11-12.

is this? Have you not heard Iamblichus saying who the two are, and making hymns to Machaon and Podalirius?" (*VP* §32)

Machaon and Podalirius are sons of Asclepius, who in their activities therefore appropriately resembled Asclepius, but also the Dioscuri. The philosopher here operates in effect as a *mantis*. The answer to the question of the identity of the God(s) in the place is a pair of discrete individuals, and there is nothing overtly philosophical, i.e., formal, in the solution, though if we examine it more closely, we can see that Machaon and Podalirius are positioned relative to the reports suggesting Asclepius and the Dioscuri respectively along the two axes of procession in Proclean henadology, insofar as they are related to Asclepius by filiation, an existential relation, and to the Dioscuri by formal resemblance, an eidetic relation.[6] Machaon and Podalirius thus account for the reported phenomena with a virtually geometric perfection, but the procedure by which Proclus obtains the result is ecstatic and mystical. This demonstrates the rigorous consistency in Proclean thought by which theophany retains its ontological priority over philosophy, while the latter retains universality as its privilege. The result is rational without being a rationalization or 'demythologization', and it never needs to leave the plane of unique, individual deities. The philosopher does not engage with the local cult as an outsider, as a superior observer who compares and assimilates, but as a participant who, if anything, excels in receptivity to the singular. The philosopher does not homogenize the local cult, but rather augments it with new relations, specifically a structure mediating diverging experiences linked to the same holy site.

We should note as well that it does not concern Marinus whether any of the people of Adratta actually adopt Proclus' solution, because his and Proclus' vision of religion is not much concerned with social control, but neither is Proclus' revelation subordinated in the interest of an 'orthopraxy' for which what is *done* is privileged over what is believed. Marinus tells us that "the God"—that is, the source of Proclus' revelation in Adratta, but who is not further identified; perhaps Machaon or Podalirius Himself;—"thought the happy man worthy of such grace that he also appeared and, in the way that one pronounces an encomium of someone in the theater, said in an actor's tone, with his hand extended in a gesture—I shall declare the very words of the God—'Proclus is the glory [*kosmos*] of the city'," (ibid., §32). It is theophany, direct and personal experience of the Gods, which is affirmed here as literally 'cosmogonic', though theophany's social and cultural context is integral to it and inseparable from it, and not merely as its occasion. Outside of the context of

---

[6] On these two axes, see "The Henadic Origin of Procession in Damascius," *Dionysius* 31 (2013), pp. 79-100.

this singular place and its religious life, nothing of Proclus' revelation would make sense or have any particular value.

This has to do with the very relationship of deities to the places sacred to them. Proclus' common term for such relations is 'allotment' or 'allocation', *lanchanein*, which expresses, for the Gods, not assignment by some other agency, but rather the limits of intelligible inquiry, which terminates, not in something beyond the Gods, but in the ineffable agency of the Gods Themselves. 'Allotment' covers for Proclus, not only the places sacred to the Gods, but even their cosmic functions; but the Gods are in no sense the passive recipients of such things. Hence, noting Plato's ambiguous usage in the *Timaeus*, in which Athena is at 23d "allotted" the guardianship of Athens and of Saïs, while at 24c she is said to have "chosen" it, *eklexamenê*, Proclus explains that

> Prior to this, the Goddess was said to have been *allotted* the Attic region, but it is now said that she *chose* it. Both, however, concur, and neither is the allotment contrary to her will, nor is her choice disorderly, as is the case with a partial soul. For divine necessity [*anankê*] concurs with divine will, choice with allotment, and *to choose* with *to be allotted*. (*IT* 1.160.26-161.1)[7]

From this perspective, there is, in effect, no 'universal' plane of divine activity that is 'localized' as if through a process of specification or speciation. Proclus speaks at times of "more universal" (*holikôteros*) and "more particular" (*merikôteros*) Gods, as notably in prop. 126 of the *Elements of Theology*, where "each is a henad, but the former has the greater potency," understood as being "the cause of more numerous effects." Proclus explains, however, that

> the more universal generate the more specific, not by division (since they are henads), nor by alteration (since they are unmoved), nor yet being multiplied by way of relation (since they transcend all relation), but by generating from themselves through surplus of potency [*dynameôs periousian*] secondary processions which are less than the prior.[8]

---

[7] *IT*: Proclus' commentary on Plato's *Timaeus*, cited according to volume, page and line numbers in E. Diehl (ed.), *Procli Diadochi In Platonis Timaeum commentaria* (Leipzig: Teubner, 1903-1906); English translation, Thomas Taylor, *Proclus' Commentary on the Timaeus of Plato* (1816) [repr. Frome, Somerset: Prometheus Trust, 1998], freely modified throughout.

[8] Proclus' *Elements of Theology* [*ET*] are cited by proposition number in E. R. Dodds (ed. & trans.), *The Elements of Theology*, 2nd ed. (Oxford: Clarendon, 1963), translations often modified.

The "surplus of potency" of prop. 126 is essentially the same, I would argue, as the "choice" spoken of in the freer terms of the *Timaeus* commentary. The term "surplus of potency" refers back to prop. 27, which establishes that production in the primary sense, and hence that which must apply to the Gods in the first place, arises from completeness (*teleiotêta*) and from surplus of potency. Completeness, however, pertains to the fulfillment of a world order,[9] whereas the henad embodies as well the surplus power of augmenting or transforming the world order to which she contributes in ways that cannot be wholly anticipated or defined by that world order; and so the henad's power beyond completeness as paradigm of a given world order is the power to choose to be *different*, and thus to choose *a different world*. 'Surplus of potency' is in fact a primitive in Proclus' system, representing a 'going beyond' inseparable from the nature of the Gods, so that the potency which is in surplus, which is going beyond, is by definition divine potency:

---

[9] 'Completion' or 'perfection' are attributes associated by Proclus with the third intelligible triad, that is, with the intellective phase of a God's activity. Cf. "The Third Intelligible Triad and the Intellective Gods," *Méthexis* 25 (2012), pp. 131-150.

a potency without all circumscription, in virtue of which the Gods have filled all things with themselves ... Thus the primary potency resides in the Gods, not dominant over a part only, but pre-embracing in itself the potencies of all beings alike; it is not a substantial potency, much less an insubstantial one, but congruent with the existence [*hyparxis*] of the Gods, supra-essential. (*ET* prop. 121)

When a God 'localizes' Herself, then, whether to a particular place or to a particular manner of worship, this procession productive of fewer effects, because they occur only in a certain place or are obtained only in certain ways, is nevertheless as much an expression of Her total nature as Her more 'universal' manifestation. The situation, in effect, is no different than the fact that a certain God chooses to operate as the *daughter* of another, and less universal in this respect than Her divine parent, but each no less a henad unlimited in power. Thus, for example, Proclus remarks concerning Athena that her first "allotment," *klēros*, is "in Her father" (*IT* 1.140.30), followed by Her activities on planes all the way down to "the place of the Earth" (ibid., 29). Choosing Zeus as Her father, therefore, is in effect Athena's first 'localization'.

What, then, constitutes the boundaries of a more 'universal' or more 'particular', or local, manifestation of a God, metaphysically speaking? The former exhibits *more powers* than the latter, and yet not, in another respect, *more power*, because divine potency by definition is "unitary" (*heniaian*) and "unencompassed" (*aperigraphos*) (*ET* prop. 121), that is, each God's potency is an infinite unit of power, and the individual potencies of the God, inasmuch as they are divine, must share this nature. Each power of a God, therefore, is in this respect an infinite potency.[10] And yet the powers of each God to some extent circumscribe one another—a problem that medieval Christian theology inherited, for example in consideration of a God's *justice* and their *mercy*. And as we have seen from *ET* prop. 126, the Gods have hierarchical relations among themselves as well of relative 'universality' and 'specificity', both between divine individuals and as a matter of processions of the same God (e.g., Zeus as universal sovereign and demiurge in the Orphic theology, while in Homer he divides the sovereignty three ways with his brothers). A God, simply *qua* God, is perfect, self-perfecting or self-completing (*autotelēs*, *ET* prop. 114); but some Gods are causes of fewer effects than others, and, as a general matter, what is "more complete is the cause of more, in proportion to the degree of its completeness ... And the less complete is the cause of less, in proportion to its incompleteness," (prop. 25). How is one to reconcile, therefore, these opposing

---

[10] Cf. my remarks on powers of the Gods in "Polytheism and Science (I): Coagulation," Noēseis, Polytheist.com, March 16, 2015, http://polytheist.com/noeseis/2015/03/16/polytheism-and-science-i-coagulation/.

senses of each God's absolute completeness and yet relative incompleteness? The key lies we may say precisely in their faculty of choice, because in completing or perfecting *themselves*, they are not completed by another, though they may in fact render themselves passive to one another or subordinate themselves one to another through choice.

If, then, the 'local' God is not merely rendered 'local' by our differential participation in Her, if that 'localizing' expresses in the first place that God's choice, then there must be a sense of *locality* appropriate to such divine action. Accordingly, Proclus explains that the "place" (*topos*) which is chosen by the God as, e.g., Athena chooses Attica, is in fact an 'interval', *diastêma*, "which is truly place; for the divisions of the divine allotments are with respect to this, in order that they may be established with eternal sameness prior to things subsisting according to time" (*IT* 1.161.1-5). *Diastêma* in this sense refers to a pure extension, the space between the boundaries of something. Aristotle considers and rejects the interval as a potential definition of place in his *Physics* (4.4, 211b), notably because "an infinite number of places would be in the same place … a place would be in another place, and many places would be together."[11] This characteristic which Aristotle finds objectionable in *diastêma* as a conception of place actually renders it peculiarly suitable for the role it plays in Proclus.

But the Gods do not choose among mere voids, like the empty coordinates on a map; an intermediary role is played by the "soul of the universe [*to pan*]," which

> possessing all the divine *logoi*, and being suspended from the things prior to it, inserts in different parts of the interval a suitability to different powers and symbols of the different classes that there are among the Gods; for this interval is immediately suspended from it [the soul of the universe] and is an instrument connascent with it. (Ibid., 5-10)

The soul of the universe, for its own part, creates general patterns of suitability in interval-space to the expression of certain divine powers and classes of Gods. Thus, for example, the passage from the *Timaeus* that occasions Proclus' comments concerns the climate of Attica, which makes it likely to bring forth people resembling Athena Herself, i.e., lovers both of war and of wisdom (*Tim.* 24c-d), which obviously involves a high degree of generality. The cooperation of the soul of the universe in the Gods' choices recognizes the continuity and integrity, the autonomy of the natural environment itself, which is not a patchwork of divine territories but rather, as Proclus says, "a rational

---

[11] *Aristotle's Physics*, trans. Hippocrates G. Apostle (Grinnell, IA: Peripatetic Press, 1980).

[*logikos*] and psychical cosmos," (*IT* 1.161.10-11) and thus has a logic of its own. But the 'place' thus chosen by a God, Proclus explains, is not

> the earth or this air, but prior to these, the unmoved interval always illuminated in the same way by the Gods, and divided by the allotments of Justice [*Dikē*]. For these material natures are sometimes fit to participate the Gods, and sometimes unfit, and it is necessary that prior to things which sometimes participate, there should be those which are always suspended in the same way from the Gods. (Ibid., 162.5-10)

This notion of the diastematic *topos*, or interval-place,[12] as it were, therefore, has far-reaching significance for our understanding of how the Gods interact with localities in the physical world. The Attica Athena chooses is not identical with the Attica in the physical world, but rather is an immaterial 'place', which coincides with physical Attica just to the degree that the latter is able, at a given moment and under given circumstances, to participate Her. By the same token, to the degree that other places in the physical world are similarly 'suitable' (*oikeios*) in general terms to the particular potencies She chooses to express through this interval or ideal diastematic place, these other physical places may be the host in the physical world of the same 'interval'. To this, we may compare the incident reported by Marinus in which Athena,

> <whose> statue, which at that time was situated in the Parthenon, was displaced by those who move even the unmoved [i.e., the Christians]. For it seemed to the philosopher in a dream that he was approached by a woman of fair aspect, who announced that he must prepare his house as quickly as possible. "For the mistress of Athens," she said, desires to live with you." (*VP* §30)

---

[12] It lies beyond the scope of the present essay to discuss the relationship between the theory of the diastematic *topoi* in the *Timaeus* commentary and Proclus' theory of space as light, which we know primarily through a passage in his commentary on the *Republic* (2.193-201 Kroll [pp. 141-51 in vol. 3 of Festugière's translation]) and from a report of his views in Simplicius' commentary on Aristotle's *Physics* (English trans. in J. O. Urmson, *Simplicius: Corollaries on Place and Time* (London: Duckworth, 1992)). The latter has been the subject of an insightful study recently by Michael Griffin, "Proclus on Place as the Luminous Vehicle of the Soul," *Dionysius* 30 (2012), pp. 161-86, though Griffin does not treat the passages discussed here from the *Timaeus* commentary. Note, however, in this respect, that Proclus' use of *diastēma* here resembles more closely that of his instructor Syrianus (in his commentary on Aristotle's *Metaphysics*, pp. 84-86 Kroll, English trans. in J. Dillon & D. O'Meara, *Syrianus: On Aristotle's Metaphysics 13-14* (Ithaca, NY: Cornell University Press, 2006), pp. 36-39) than his own later theory.

We may note here Marinus' interesting use of the term 'unmoved'. The place of Athena's statue on the Parthenon, when understood not physically alone but devotionally too, is an immovable diastematic *topos*. The Christians remove the statue to a place where it cannot participate Her in the same way, separating it, in their impiety, from its participation in its diastematic place and treating it as a mere statue. By this very act of separation from its physical place, the diastematic or interval-place comes into correspondence with a different place in the physical world. Nothing about this process, we must recognize, is exclusive; everything naturally participates the Gods in all the ways and with whatever capacities or to whatever degree it is capable at any given time. There are obviously ways in which the physical space of the Parthenon, not to mention the natural environment of the region, would continue to participate in Athena's activity, and ways in which the statue, removed to a new location, continued to participate in Her activity as well, in addition to the new participation instituted by the Goddess and made possible by the suitable conditions of the philosopher's home.

In this fashion, "the same place is at different times occupied by different spirits," and while certain "sacred rites [are] dissolved" (*IT* 1.139.18-20), the aptitude "produced by nature as a whole" (26) spontaneously ensures that in such a place "divinity reveals itself … that was previously concealed through the inaptitude of the recipients, possessing eternally its proper allotment, and always extending participation in itself, but not always being received," (140.5-8). It is not a matter, here, of introducing a providential order into the tragedies of history and the follies and crimes of human beings; rather, Proclus compares the situation to that of mortal souls choosing different lives at different times (140.9-22), and who may choose a life "in forgetfulness of the [Gods] proper to them" (11) or have such a life chosen for them, to some degree, by political forces (15-18), which affects the "rectitude" and success of their works (18-22; again at 163.30-164.10). But even if a place may, as a result, produce "fewer wise persons … having fallen away from a life adapted to the place" (164.12-15), the Gods, nevertheless, are everywhere.

Finally, and on a more speculative note, 'interval' or 'extension' seems so formal or abstract a sense of place that it cannot be limited in its expression to physical places, but must apply to any division[13] of spacetime. This is just as much limitation as is provided by the close association of *diastēma* with the soul

---

[13] Strictly speaking, Proclus would say that place is indivisible (*adiaireton*, e.g., at Simplicius, *In Aristotelis Physicorum* 612.16); however, at *IT* 1.161.2-3, he says that the divisions (*diaireseis*) of the divine allotments are with respect to [*kata*] this, i.e. *diastēma*, which is place in the truest sense. Perhaps Proclus would say that just as the 'more particular' henad is not a division of the 'more universal', the interval-place has not arisen from division but as a direct divine production, which would explain why a virtually inexhaustible multiplicity of such 'divisions' exists.

of the universe as its 'instrument' (*organon*), and which serves to distinguish this sense of place from that which applies to the higher plane of intelligible-intellective activity of the Gods, in which primary *topoi* are given which I have characterized as 'pantheon space', and which are prior to spacetime altogether.[14] The 'place' of things in the primary psychical sense, however, coming after the plane of intellective formation, applies to ensouled beings and expresses the embeddedness of things in the total lived experience or continuum of space and time. The 'places' in question, therefore, could be positions as much historical as geographical, and this in diverse ways and on diverse planes. Hence, a 'local' cult could be *local* in any of a number of senses: local to a physical place; to a certain time, whether in linear, unrepeatable time or in cyclical time; or local to a certain *soul* or group of souls,[15] without reference to physical space or, potentially, time. Already in Proclus' time, Christian oppression had forced many cults to be practiced by solitary individuals or by small groups, and often no longer in association with traditional cult sites. Today's polytheists, by virtue of the possibilities technology affords, may form cultic associations without physical proximity either to such sites, or of the members to one another. Moreover, we may regard modern polytheists in this sense as not 'reviving' or 'reconstructing' ancient cults, but as actually participating in the same 'intervals' of spacetime as those cults. Hence the 'local' may be conceptualized so broadly as to encompass locality in spacetime, but not be limited to this type of locality—an effort to which the Platonic conceptual framework shows itself remarkably well suited.[16]

What can we say in conclusion about the relationship of the philosopher to this localizing faculty of the Gods? The philosopher, in occupying the position of universality in just the way she does, plays a role relative to the diverse theologies very much like that which the One Itself plays with respect to the Gods. Just as the One, far from being an anticipation of the One God of the monotheists, actually preserves inviolate, through its rigorous negativity, the

---

[14] See "The Second Intelligible Triad and the Intelligible-Intellective Gods," *Méthexis* 23 (2010), pp. 137-157.
[15] Cf. the reference to a "distribution according to the determinate vehicles of souls" at *IT* 1.139.12-13.
[16] A 'local cult' may be defined without any controlling reference to spacetime as follows: a local cult is composed entirely of primary sites of divine election (i.e., places, times, souls). The next degree of universality, 'regional' cult, in the sense used by R. Werbner, *Regional Cults* (London: Academic Press, 1977), would be a cult in which there is a primary differentiation of persons (or places, times, et al.) and functions permitting the authorized formal extension of the primary cultic 'place'. Further degrees of formalization yield further degrees of 'universality' approaching a vanishing point of empty formality identical with existence as such.

polytheist field, so too, the philosopher holds the place of the totality of Gods and of pantheons, not in the name of any positive theology, but precisely so that no theology may annex to itself the space common to them all. Philosophy, though a quintessentially mortal discipline and ontologically subordinate to revelation, possesses by virtue of that very subordination a universality without constraint. The philosopher must hold to the universality specific to philosophy, for it is to philosophy, rather than to theology, that polytheism in the absolutely unrestricted sense appears, inasmuch as there is no *universal pantheon*, any more than there is a pantheon peculiar to philosophy: these two facts entail one another. The philosopher's universality, inasmuch as it consists in a radical openness to the peculiarity of individual Gods, expresses the nature of henadic totality, which is grounded, not in the wholeness of a pantheon, in which each God plays their part, but in the immediate presence of each God to all things.

> Edward Butler received his doctorate from the New School for Social Research in 2004 for his dissertation "The Metaphysics of Polytheism in Proclus." Since then, he has published numerous articles in academic journals and edited volumes, primarily on Platonism and Neoplatonism and on polytheistic philosophy of religion. He also writes Noēseis, a regular column for Polytheist.com, and is on the editorial board of *Walking the Worlds*. More information about his work can be found on his site, Henadology: Philosophy and Theology (henadology. wordpress.com). His article in this issue, "Time and the Heroes," continues the work on Proclus begun in his dissertation and in the articles collected and republished in his *Essays on the Metaphysics of Polytheism* (New York City: Phaidra Editions, 2014).

Syncretism as Methodology of Localization: A Short Note on Antinoan Cultus in Antiquity and in the Syncretistic Present

P. SUFENAS VIRIUS LUPUS

This short article addresses the manner in which the majority of attested cultus to the super-syncretistic late antique Graeco-Roman-Egyptian hero/deity Antinous—apart from his syncretisms to Hermes, Dionysos, and Apollon—are not witnessed outside of extremely limited localities. Almost every syncretized form of Antinous is, therefore, a "local god" for that particular syncretistic epiphany. Some degree of the place-specific landscape and character of more widely-attested syncretistic deities comes through in their localized forms, and there is no reason to think this will not continue with Antinous (and, by extension, other deities, super-syncretistic or not) in the modern polytheistic context, particularly by the extension of the corpus of mythological narratives to cover the presence of a deity and their worshippers in new diasporic locations where their cultus may have been hitherto unattested.

Two of the ways in which syncretism seemed to function in the ancient Mediterranean and European worlds were either as an "equation" of two different deities or divine beings (both across pantheons, e.g. Jupiter Dolichenus or Persephone-Ereshkigal, and within pantheons, e.g. Apollon-Paion, Eos-Hemera, etc.), or as a "translation" of them,[1] the latter of which has been unappreciated and often ignored as a possibility within both scholarship on the ancient world and on practical and devotional engagements with deities. Whether this is due to an assumed superiority of a monistic theology over the inherent and necessary pluralism required within polytheism, or some other factor, probably depends as widely on the individual evaluators concerned as on any other wide-ranging explanation of the phenomenon. Nonetheless, the possibility of syncretism as translation is also given in a slightly different form in the work of Edward Butler, where the concept of "polycentric polytheism" makes it possible, by virtue of deities being deities, that they can contain the divine potentials of all other deities within themselves, and thus one deity can

---

[1] See P. Sufenas Virius Lupus, *A Serpent Path Primer* (Anacortes: The Red Lotus Library, 2012), pp. 9-11.

easily act in the role of another without creating a necessary equation between them, nor in any other manner muddying the waters between their two separate and distinct identities.[2]

Where certain deities are concerned, a phenomenon that I have referred to as "super-syncretism" also occurs,[3] in which a deity like Serapis, Isis, Mithras, or a variety of others seems to absorb the divine attributes of many other deities in a promiscuous fashion, without likewise absorbing or subsuming the individual identities of those other deities. This, likewise, has often resulted in the characterization of these types of deities as "pantheistic,"[4] but I would argue this reading is overstated, as the combination of *many* deities does not necessarily imply the inclusion of *every* deity. Again, the overstatement in these cases may simply be a reflection of the tendency of some commentators to mistake "some" or even "many" for "all," which seems to be a difficulty for a variety of people who have become habituated to thinking that any number of deities more than one (or more than three-in-one) is somehow a confusing jumble that cannot possibly have been discriminated by the "less-advanced" peoples of the past, which by no means is necessitated by the evidence or our interpretations of it.

One case of super-syncretism which brings many of these issues to clearer light is that of Antinous, the deified lover of the Roman Emperor Hadrian, who was syncretized to a large variety of Greek, Roman, and Egyptian deities and heroes in his attested late antique cultus.[5] An active translational syncretism seems to be the *modus operandi* of his cultus, as the vast number of these attested syncretized forms are profoundly localized and are not otherwise attested. Hermes, Dionysos, and Apollon seem to be widely-appearing syncretisms for Antinous, but these are the exceptions rather than the rule.[6]

Clearly, no one in the ancient world would have argued that Antinous was "equal to" or "replaced" a given deity, either locally or on a more cosmic, metaphysical, or theological level. Thus, these syncretized forms of Antinous may be viewed as manners via which his more widespread and "international" cultus was made local, familiar, and in essence "domesticated" and enculturated to a given location. It would thus be no surprise that he was Osiris-Antinous

---

[2] Edward Butler, "'Polycentric Polytheism and the Philosophy of Religion," *The Pomegranate: The International Journal of Pagan Studies* 10.2 (2008), pp. 207-229.

[3] Lupus, *Serpent Path*, pp. 47-54.

[4] As, for example, with Sabazios, e.g. Robert Turcan, *The Cults of the Roman Empire*, trans. Antonia Nevill (Oxford: Blackwell, 1996), pp. 315-326; or with Tithoes/Tutu, e.g. Olaf E. Kaper, *The Egyptian God Tutu: A Study of the Sphinx-God and Master of Demons with a Corpus of Monuments* (Louvain: Peeters, 2003).

[5] For more on the most common attestations of these, see Lupus, *The Syncretisms of Antinous* (Anacortes: The Red Lotus Library, 2010).

[6] Lupus, *Syncretisms*, pp. 14-27.

only in Antinoöpolis and in the Egyptianized Antinoeion, his tomb and temple at Hadrian's Villa,[7] but not in Athens; that he was Poseidon-Antinous in Corinth[8] but not in Mantineia; that he was Silvanus-Antinous in Lanuvium[9] but not in Syria; and that he was Echmoun-Antinous in Leptis Magna[10] but not in Bithynia. In both his home territory of Bithynia, as well as in Mantineia—the Arcadian polis which was the mother city-state for the colony where he was born—he is referred to as *Epichorios Theos*, "the local/native god";[11] to an extent, therefore, any syncretized form of Antinous could be understood as "the local god" wherever his cultus might be found.

Other instances of widespread deities in world religions who have established localized syncretisms are, for example, the various localized forms of the Blessed Virgin Mary in Roman Catholicism (e.g. the Virgin of Guadalupe, Our Lady of Fátima, Our Lady of Lourdes, etc.), where in some cases the attributes of local indigenous goddesses are combined with the more widely-attested divine feminine figure. As very few late antique deities had the chance to spread further than the Mediterranean and European worlds, we cannot be certain how this would have worked if colonists from a polytheist culture would have reached further afield in Africa, Asia, or even to the Americas, Australia, and Oceania.

This variety of translational syncretism, and the emergence of polycentric polytheist treatments of (figuratively) diasporic deities when they arrive and become incorporated into a local landscape and populace presents both a challenge and an opportunity to the modern student of and adherent to polytheist religious practices. Firstly, it is a challenge to any examination of a localized cultus of any deity from the ancient world to discern not only the more widespread and international character of a deity in any location where they have become a resident in their honoring (e.g. Mars in Roman Britian), but also what indigenous elements in that location have been brought to bear on their cultus—whether epithets or titles, functions, narratives, inherited practices, or any other characteristics. Second, it is an ongoing challenge as well as an opportunity for modern practitioners, who are often outside of the indigenous areas where various deities have been worshipped, to seek to seat their deities in their local landscape and its own traditions, while likewise being aware that

---

[7] Lupus, *Syncretisms*, pp. 28-32.
[8] Lupus, *Syncretisms*, pp. 53-56.
[9] Lupus, *Syncretisms*, pp. 37-40.
[10] Lupus, *Syncretisms*, pp. 140-142.
[11] Hugo Meyer, *Antinoos: Die archäologischen Denkmäler unter Einbeziehung des numismatischen und epigraphischen Materials sowie der literarischen Nachrichten, Ein Beitrag zur Kunst- und Kulturgeschichte der hadrianisch-frühantoninischen Zeit* (Munich: Wilhelm Fink, 1991), pp. 166-167.

cultural appropriation is never permissible nor a viable option in pursuing this process.

For the modern Antinoan devotee and practitioner, it can be assumed that the super-syncretistic tendencies of the past will not have ceased with the ostensible "triumph" of Christianity in late antiquity; but even beyond these tendencies, any deity who ends up in a diasporic situation will of necessity become localized in some fashion or other. As a set of brief case studies in this phenomenon, we might ask ourselves: what might the Antinoan cultus have become in locations where it did not historically reach, and with which divine beings might Antinous have become syncretized if he had reached those locations?[12] While the possibilities in this regard are quite boundless, some divine beings seem more likely than others to have been candidates for such translational syncretisms, polycentric polytheist theophanies, and methods for localization. For present purposes, it might be suggested that Antinous' cultus, had it reached ancient Germania, may have entailed syncretisms with Freyr (a chthonic deity associated with fertility and also with drowning, characteristics shared with Antinous), Mani (a god of the moon, which is a common association with Antinous, and the source of his syncretism to the Phrygian moon god Men, linguistically and mythically cognate to Mani), and/or Baldr (a superlatively beautiful deity with a tragic death); if it had reached Ireland, perhaps Cú Chulainn (a hero who died young, and also had power over the rising of rivers); in India, Skanda (a youthful and often unmarried deity, who shares many characteristics with Dionysos—a common Antinoan syncretism— and who was finally born from the Ganges River) and Hanuman (in a fashion comparable to the Hindu deity of devotion's relationship to Ram and Sita, suggested by Antinous' intercession on his Obelisk for Hadrian and Sabina) seem likely candidates; and in Japan, Sarutahiko-no-Okami (a Hermes-like deity of guidance and guardianship who was said to have drowned in the *Kojiki*) might be a possibility.

However, what would the dynamics of these syncretisms—novel and modern or attested from the ancient world—be when the cultus of Antinous takes root in new lands, like the Americas? Would deities indigenous to the cultures from those areas likewise syncretize with Antinous? Might it be

---

[12] While it may seem naïve to do so, let us assume that this might not have taken place because of the worldwide expansion of the Roman Empire, but instead was due to the travel and trading contacts between disparate cultures, who may have found something of appeal in him and brought his cultus back with them to their own locations. Indeed, this seems to have been how his cultus spread within the Roman Empire, as there were no known "missionaries" promulgating his cultus abroad, nor were there imperial officials charged with setting up his cultus in diverse locations for some wider goal in mind, whether spiritual or political, that Hadrian or other Antinoan devotees may have had.

possible that Tlaloc, Coyote,[13] or other divine beings might syncretize with him? Unless there are direct contacts between modern devotees of Antinous and representatives of these cultures, and the latter perhaps develop devotional relationships of their own and begin this intercultural connection under their own initiative, to simply begin suggesting potential mythic and cultic parallels would be inadvisable at best, and actively culturally appropriative at worst.

The more essential question would be: how do the indigenous deities of Europe and the wider Mediterranean basin land and settle in North America and other places with the diasporic European polytheists and pagans who revere them? How can this be done in ways that are respectful, and which are always actively mindful of the atrocities that European colonization, enslavement, and cultural genocide have enacted upon the peoples of these lands?

While theological syncretism can be one way in which new or imported deities can become localized to new places, a second method might be preferable in the context of North and South America particularly. Mythological syncretism rather than theological syncretism may be a strong and viable possibility for how this could be done. Just as Herakles' wanderings of the world made sense of his far-flung cultus, including his syncretism to Near Eastern deities like Melqart in Iberia, so too could new tales of the wanderings of Antinous—or indeed any other deity—be a way to seek connection of deities from other continents to lands their older cultus never reached, without suggesting that they have taken up permanent residence in those cultures in a divine echo of the theft and appropriation of indigenous peoples' territories.

Narrative is a natural method via which certain cultural elements have spread across continents, in antiquity and more recently, and in which every human culture shares a great interest. A new generation of epic and lyric poets, storytellers, and commentators and glossators must take up the mantle of our ancient literary forebears and begin to create myths—explanatory as well as exemplary in nature—as to how the deities of the ancient and medieval European and Mediterranean worlds came into contact with the lands and peoples of the Americas, modeling how this can be done in a pious and respectful fashion in order to instill these same values in the modern peoples who likewise must exist within a legacy of gross cultural injustices. Where humans have transgressed, our deities and the inspiration they can provide through new myths might be a way to not only come to terms with these intercultural disasters, but also to allow us as modern people aware of these situations to more authentically respect the lands and peoples of the Americas

---

[13] A Native American that I was in contact with during the start of my own Antinoan practice suggested Coyote as a likely North American syncretism due to Coyote's tendency to shapeshift, which he interpreted as what occurred with Antinous' prolific syncretism.

and thus become welcome guests in these places rather than unwanted intruders.

> P. Sufenas Virius Lupus is a metagender person, and the *Doctor, Magistratum, Mystagogos, Sacerdos,* and one of the founding members of the Ekklesía Antínoou—a queer, Graeco-Roman-Egyptian syncretist reconstructionist polytheist group dedicated to Antinous, the deified lover of the Roman Emperor Hadrian, and related deities and divine figures—as well as a contributing member of Neos Alexandria and a practicing Celtic Reconstructionist pagan in the traditions of *gentlidecht* and *filidecht*, as well as Romano-British, Welsh, and Gaulish deity devotions. Lupus is also dedicated to several land spirits around the area of North Puget Sound and its islands. Lupus' work (poetry, fiction, and essays) has appeared in a number of Bibliotheca Alexandrina devotional volumes, as well as Ruby Sara's anthologies *Datura* (2010) and *Mandragora* (2012), Inanna Gabriel and C. Bryan Brown's *Etched Offerings* (2011), Lee Harrington's *Spirit of Desire: Personal Explorations of Sacred Kink* (2010), Galina Krasskova's *When the Lion Roars* (2011), Tara Miller's *Rooted in the Body, Seeking the Soul* (2013), Sarenth Odinsson's *Calling to Our Ancestors* (2015), and Crystal Blanton, Taylor Ellwood and Brandy Williams' *Bringing Race to the Table* (2015), as well as various esoteric, Pagan and polytheist periodicals. Lupus has also written several full-length books, including *The Phillupic Hymns* (2008), *The Syncretisms of Antinous* (2010), *Devotio Antinoo: The Doctor's Notes, Volume One* (2011), *All-Soul, All-Body, All-Love, All-Power: A TransMythology* (2012), *A Garland for Polydeukion* (2012), *A Serpent Path Primer* (2012), and *Ephesia Grammata: Ancient History and Modern Practice* (2014), with more on the way. Lupus blogs at Aedicula Antinoi (aediculaantinoi.wordpress.com), and also has the "Speaking of Syncretism" column at polytheist.com.

Sea, Earth, and What Came of It: Devotional Practice on the Information Ocean

RAVEN KALDERA

> A shaman called to perform a series of devotional acts for a family of sea deities eventually begins constructing online shrines for them and others. These "virtual" spaces of worship not only resonate with the devotees who use them, but find favor with the deities who are honored, resulting in deeper spiritual relationships offline as well.

It all started because I love the ocean, and I've almost always lived within a couple of hours of a coast. As a child, my parents took us to the beach off and on throughout the summer, and I loved it there. The waves spoke to me, and to this day the smell of salt air makes a feeling of elation course through my veins. Just immersing myself in seawater made many of my chronic ailments recede. It always seemed like another world to me, a doorway to a magical realm I couldn't enter, but could watch from afar.

As an adult Pagan, I knew theoretically about many sea gods and goddesses – Poseidon, Neptune, Mariamne, Sedna, Llyr, Dewi, Tiamat – but none of them really seemed to touch me. It might also have been that none of them cared to be more than a distant figure, because my connection to the sea was already spoken for; I just didn't know by whom. At any rate, the ocean was still magical; I just didn't connect it to Deity the way that I walked with Herne in the forest and the North Wind through the snowstorm.

For all my love of the ocean, however, the element of Water has always seemed the most elusive to me. From an astrological perspective, Water is emotion, and I've always been the sort of person who is more focused on doing than feeling. I'm not comfortable with feelings, in general, and I tend to ignore them whenever possible. (I am only just now, in my later years, beginning to come to terms with those parts of myself.) The modern Neo-Pagan view of Water tends to emphasize its flowing, healing, peaceful qualities, and thus I instinctively avoided it; as someone mostly chosen by gods of Death and Storm and Fire, I'm just not much of a flowing, healing, peaceful person. I know now that in order to fully understand an element, I need to start with its most destructive qualities – just as, in order to fully honor a deity, I need to understand their dark side.

Fortunately, the Northern Tradition is all about facing down the destructive side of the elements. The proverbial tension between differing pantheons in this tradition comes, at bottom, from the tension between Civilization – that which is convenient to human beings – and Wild Nature, which by definition is not. In my religious tradition, the context of my shamanic practice, Fire is that which burns down forests, Earth is the mountain that flings boulders in the quake, Air is the winter blizzard....and Water is the ocean that eats you.

"Mastering the elements," in my shamanic tradition, is not about getting power over them. (Frankly, that idea is so hubristic as to be ridiculous.) Rather, it is the process of learning their mysteries, and making alliances with whichever spirits choose to work with you. It is also a process that spirals upwards rather than proceeding in a straight line - you learn a little about each one, then over time a little more, and so forth. I'd gone through the "basic" training for Fire, Air, and Earth, and I faced down Water with some trepidation. I didn't even know who – or Who – to call on. All the deities I'd worked with before were Beings of fire or wind or harvest....or, usually, darkness. Yet as I sat there pondering, I heard a faint call, like the sound of waves. "Come to us," they said. Multiple voices, all female. "Come to us and we'll teach you the mysteries of Water," they said. "The real ones."

So I took two weeks and made a pilgrimage to the Atlantic Ocean, seeing it from the perspective of nine different beaches. At each one I made an offering of song and gifts, and walked into the water as deep as I dared, and one of the Sisters rose up each time and spoke to me. Each one of them taught me a different mystery of Water, on a visceral rather than an intellectual level. While I won't deny that Water is still the most elusive element, I now have an understanding of it at a blood-deep (not bone-deep, bone is Earth) level, and I feel much more comfortable with it.

The Nine Sisters, also known as the Nine Waves, are the daughters of Aegir and Ran, the Norse King and Queen of the ocean. Unlike the kindly Norse god Njord whose care is ships and sailing and fisherfolk – the use of an element for the benefit of man rather than the wild element itself – this family of goddesses (and one father-god) is neither kindly nor pretty. In fact, some of the sisters insist that I refrain from using modern "pretty" mermaid pictures for them – they are untamed, fierce, uncontrollable deities with claws and fangs, teeth like undersea predators and ropes of broken shells in their tangled manes. They are the embodiment of the ocean that eats you....and yet they can be kind to you, if they like you. I no longer have any fear of drowning, now that I know them. I simply need to appreciate them for what they are, and not expect them to be some human ideal of an all-giving Barbie-doll goddess.

There was icy Kolga, the Sister of the frozen Arctic waters, who taught the mystery of Cold, and its uses. There was her twin Duva, who name means Hidden, the lady of mists and islands who can save sailors or leave them to drown, and who peeled back a corner of her veil to show me the depths. There was Hronn the Whirlpool Goddess who ruled the watery nature of Fear, and her twin Hevring the Mourning Mermaid whose unending sorrow sees what we humans have done to the seas. There was bounding Bylgja riding the wave-horse, who dares us to challenge the energy of the shoreline waves and risk being carried away in the breakers. There was enormous Bara the Whale-Goddess, Lady of the Tsunami, who delights in every bit of dry land that is reclaimed by the ocean. There was mysterious Unn who rules tides and seabirds and can move forward and backward through Time, and the elusive Himinglava, the Fair-Weather Goddess whose name means Sun Shining Through. The first one of the Sisters to approach me, however, was Blodughadda – the Bloody-Haired One – who bore the fin and tail of a shark and taught me her mysteries of Blood – which, after all, is very similar to seawater in its composition, for a good reason.

I won't go into everything I learned from them in this article, because I wrote it down and published it in a number of places. In spite of my writings, I figured that my relationship with them was wholly personal; in other words, that I would probably be the only one who ever talked to them, except for other accidental beach-walkers who caught their eye and were psychically sensitive enough to bother approaching. But when I spoke to a dear friend about it, she became excited. She lived near a beach on the Pacific Ocean, thousands of miles from my Atlantic tidepools, and had something of a relationship with Ran because of it. She'd had encounters that she couldn't quite explain, but my description of the Sisters clicked, and she began to honor them in her own spiritual work. We joked about how we two were the keepers of the Cult of the Nine Sisters – one on each coast, like eastern and western lighthouses of their worship – and when she eventually died some years later, I felt as if our little cultus had been half cast into shadow.

The Sisters gave me solace, strength, and sometimes helped me with my healing. I wanted to give something back to them besides just the regular offerings I threw into the ocean every summer (ocean-wildlife-safe, of course), so I organized a yearly group ritual among friends in my Pagan church who liked the idea. The first year – and every year since – I dowsed on a map to see where on the New England coast the Sisters wanted us to go. (Somewhere with a public parking lot, please!) My pendulum went crazy over Bailey Island, off the coast of Maine, but I wasn't sure about where to go once we were there. I kidded about how we should drive there and drive around until we saw the right place, but didn't really mean to do that. Then I did a search on Bailey Island and discovered that it had a public beach composed of great rocky cliffs called the Giants' Stairs. (The Nine Sisters and their parents are often referred to as "giants" or "giant-gods," largely denoting that they were probably part of the older pre-Indo-European deity complex.) So yes, theoretically, we could have gone there and wandered around until we saw the sign for that beach.

As it was, we had our sea faining, ceremonially called them, and they came. We felt their presences all around us as the sea reared up joyously and smote the rocks, spilling the basket of fruit that was our offering and playfully dunking a few of us, but harming none. Since then we've done our yearly faining at different beaches every year between Canada and Connecticut, each one chosen by them via dowsing.

However, the Sisters can also be thanked for pushing me to a devotional act on a larger scale. I'd built them a floating altar – a mobile made of driftwood hung with shells, sea floats, dried fish, and other ocean trinkets – but they told me that they wanted a shrine *where everyone could see it*. I thought about building something at some seaside property, but couldn't figure out a way to keep that going safely. Instead, I turned to the Internet, the great ocean of information. I built them an online shrine bedecked with descriptions of them, devotional poetry, copyright-free ocean photos….and, eventually, donated artwork and writing from others who were working with them. My junior partner the tech geek set up a system whereby people could light "virtual candles," posting their prayers anonymously.

The shrine was up barely a week on our new website, www.northern-paganism.org, when we began to receive emails praising it, thanking us for introducing them to the Nine, and begging us to put up online shrines to other Norse/Germanic deities. At the same time, I was getting pokes both from Gods I knew well and Gods who hardly spoke to me, asking for online shrines of their own. Over the next three years we put up shrines full of poetry, rituals, writing, original artwork, and candles for sending up prayers to eighty-eight northern Gods, plus a shrine to the Ancestors. We weren't sure about this at first – I figured that the shrines would be, like so many other odd websites, online occasional tourist attractions of the "world's largest ball of string" variety. My partner was skeptical about the virtual candles, seeing them as sort of hokey compared to actual in-front-of-your-altar devotion.

Instead, the response has been amazing, and heart-warming. As the online "temple keeper" who gets to see the anonymous prayers being posted, I am moved almost to tears on a weekly basis by the beauty and devotion of the words that are posted. Some are simple pleas for help – heal or protect me or this family member, help us find a new home, lay your hand over this cause or that person – and some are words of praise so personal and spontaneous that it is obvious that the writers had created their own relationship with that deity, based on the writings of others found on the site. I also know that this is true because people email me and thank me for introducing them to this obscure god or that obscure goddess, of whom they never would have known without these highly accessible sites. One woman wrote about how she tries to light a candle to at least one of the Gods during her lunch hour at work. It really made

> **THE CAULDRON magazine**
> Traditional Witchcraft, Wicca,
> Paganism and Folklore
>
> Four issues $50.00 by check payable to
> M.A. Howard sent to BM Cauldron, London
> WC1N 3XX, England, United Kingdom
> or by PayPal at our website
> **www.the-cauldron.org.uk**

me see the websites as the modern equivalent of the roadside shrine, tucked away along the information highway. Even my skeptical partner has now completely come around, and sees the website maintenance as just another part of our sacred work in the world. We've now finished with the Norse/Germanic gods, and are tentatively beginning a site with shrines for deities from other pantheons, but since these are not my Gods I've decided to require sponsors – someone to write the main text and description – for future shrines. We'll see how this works out.

The shrine story that most touched my heart, however, is one not of Water but of Earth – specifically Jord, the Norse Earth Mother (and the mother of Thor and Frigga). I put up an online shrine to her almost routinely, more to be complete than anything else. It was simple – few people honor Jord with anything more than the occasional naming or food offering, and there were only a few prayers and poems – but it was there, and soon anonymous candles appeared extolling Earth and its beauty.

Later that month, I got in the car with my junior partner and our dog and drove to West Virginia for a conference where I was presenting. This trip is normally done ninety percent on the highway, but for some reason our GPS suddenly decided to tell us to take some long, winding, back routed road for a hundred miles instead, all across the top of West Virginia. (Our transmission did not like the steep hills at all.) After a few miles, a deer ran across the road and we braked to miss it. Then another one a few miles down. Then another one. Then a *dead* deer by the side of the road. Then a doe and fawn, standing there by the roadside and watching us.

At this point, I was thinking, "This is ceasing to be a deer-season coincidence," and my partner said, "Um, if someone is trying to tell you something, you'd better figure out what to do before I accidentally hit something live," I agreed that I should probably stop, and ask. But where to stop? It was all fenced pasture and houses." Then, bang, in less than a minute we came upon a state park. An empty state park. We turned off, my partner took the dog for a run, and I sat on a stump and asked, "Zup, Guys?"

It was Jord. Her visage rose up out of the earth in front of me, dragging the local land-spirit with her. Now I have a really hard time with trips away, even though I love to travel, because I have a chronic illness and I depend on our land-spirit to give me energy to help keep me well, and being away I often get sick. I've tried bringing dirt with me to keep under the pillow in hotel rooms (thus inspiring many "vampires and native earth" jokes from roommates), but it only gives me a little thread of energy. Jord dragged the land-spirit over and ordered it to feed me, which it did, and then lumbered off. She was big and round and brown and beautiful and she said, "Anywhere you go, if you can find a piece of wild land, I will make the land-spirit feed you."

And I asked why, in bewilderment, and she said, "You made me a shrine. No one has ever made me a shrine before. Ever. They put offerings into the earth, but never a shrine. So don't worry about getting fed through the land when you travel – I'll take care of it."

I was so happy, I cried for half an hour. And getting this crusty old Hel's man to cry for half an hour, that's something. It was an amazing lesson in gratitude - not just the immense gratitude that we can experience when we have been helped by the Gods, but that the gifts we offer them are not thrown into a void. The Gods care, and they show that caring if we're willing to notice it.

Is this regional cultus? Can the Internet be considered a "region"? Surely it is growing its own various cultures; is it so impossible that the Gods would move people to find a way to honor them in this strange country of its own? Some may scoff at the idea that a computer script with a digital candle image would count the same as making real flame while kneeling in front of a box or shelf full of real objects….but Jord apparently thinks it does, and I see more proof in the prayers that appear every day on my little virtual temple. "Please, Holda, help us to find the right house that we can afford!" "Holda, the house is beautiful, thank you so much!" It's not the medium, it's the message, and the emotion behind it. This is the core of devotion, not the forms which are simply interchangeable containers. This – the personal experience – is why these evolve at all, in the end.

> Raven Kaldera is a northern Tradition shaman, writer, herbalist, homesteader, and activist. To learn more, visit ravenkaldera.org. "Tis an ill wind that blows no minds."

Awakening the Land: Madness and the Return of Welsh Gods

RHYD WILDERMUTH

Through exploring the madness of Bards and Awenyddion, the secret of re-enchantment unfolds through the land itself and the Gods clothed in forest and mountain.

"Around the world, discontent can be heard. The extremists are grinding their knives and moving in as the machine's coughing and stuttering exposes the inadequacies of the political oligarchies and who claimed to have everything in hand. Old gods are rearing their heads, and old answers: revolution, war, ethnic strife."[1]

I.

To know a god, you must go mad.

We call it dis-enchantment, this sallow state of existence, the frayed-threads of the tapestry of meaning. Modernity we call it, and freedom, progress and arrival into a future without them.

Once Them. Once us. Them with us. We with them.

Now--cut. Wounds cauterized in the searing heat of machined-mills, branches severed below the fork, roots encased in concrete, veins of memory collapsed.

We are disenchanted, disinherited, dis-tracted, led away, leaden feet sinking into grey dust of barren lands which cannot soak up the water falling from heavy, pregnant skies.

Scrambling up wet scree tumbling down upon iron rails, boots sodden, fingers pricked through upon needle of gorse, I climbed to ask them for help. One loomed far south of me, scraggly hair, unbearded, watching the man far below pretend comfort with heights. Behind and below, across the tracks and further in the snow-melt swollen river, the indifferent guardian waited, waited like water waits.

"Okay," I shouted, dizzied, guessing how long it'd take my companion to find my broken-necked corpse on the tracks. Would he find me before the train? Or likely find me after, even more mangled.

---

[1] Paul Kingsnorth and Dougald Hine, *The Dark Mountain Manifesto*

"Okay. I—uh. I'm actually—I can't climb anymore. Can we talk from here?"

Laughter, amusement, felt through the stone, shaking the rain.

"Ah...good. Sorry. I'm actually a really small person, and I don't think I can reach that rock and—yeah. So."

Attempts at formality would look more false than my bravado. They already know who I am, why I'm there. If the guardian in the river hadn't told them, the gate-hound would have, and even if they'd held their tongue, they're kin of him I'm there for. And I've no composure for pretense, a hundred-foot drop below my slipping grip.

"I was wondering if you'd help me?"

More laughter. Assent shouted through bone.

"Ah. Okay. Thanks!" Suddenly seemed easy. Giants are good-natured, after all, even the child-slaying and beard-flaying ones. I almost let go the exposed tree-root which kept me from falling the hundred feet to rails below, so relieved I was.

Their laughter continued. The Fool's often amusing, and I near laughed with them, noticing my predicament. I couldn't get down.

"Stride down like us," I heard, with voice clearer than through ears. "And give her our gift."

My boots are wet. I'm wet. Shirtless, covered in mud, hanging by roots and rocks. I am the water pouring down my skin, I'm soaking through myself into the rock and becoming the lake at the source of the river, and he's coming. They're there.

You don't have to go mad to see them, but you must abandon reason to keep them around after the sight. Giants, nymphs, ghosts—they're there, you've seen them maybe once but then looked away and forgot. Shaking off and away the vision, looking again, changing your view so they're not there on the second glance. Dis-enchanted.

We don't do this just with The Other, we do this with ourselves, particularly with desire. The Other is queer, sometimes we are, and like the man denying desire for another man in a world where only women are allowed, The Other is the queer we disallow. Easier to deny different desire when surrounded by others who also deny; easier to disallow god-giants when no-one else admits to them.

To dis-allow is to forbid; to dis-enchant is to de-ny, repudiate, withhold from ourselves what we thought occurred. Self-abnegation, sacrificial poverty of spirit so we can be what we're supposed to be, what is demanded of us. Resist the trembling lust for what your flesh desires and nothing queer enters into the world of self-controlled workers selling time for money.

Money is extracted time, he shouted at me, and I shook. I shook like the time he pushed me back, wouldn't let me pass. I tried, he pushed again. I pushed back. Don't get in a pushing match with a giant.

I shook like the time he was in my head, rummaging there, sifting, sorting. "Who's this?" he said, one of the few times I've heard his voice with my ears.

"Just someone I desired," I answered, and he shook his head.

II.

We're drunk. I'm drunker, but he's pretty drunk too.
"Who's Brad?"
We're naked. We're usually naked when we sleep, and we're usually together when we sleep.
"Brad?" I'm drunk. I forgot who Brad is. There was Brett, a couple of Brians or at least one Brian and one Bryan.
"He must've been damn good."

We just became whatever we are. Lovers? Sort of, partners, boyfriends— why we need names I don't know. And I'm hoping to keep this one around. He's a good one, actually. Shrugged when he saw my altar. I'm not the first pagan he's been with, not even the first pagan writer. First pagan writer-guy, though. That's something.

But I'm drunk and I don't know who he's talking about.

"I—I don't know a Brad." I'm pretty certain of this. I'm actually pretty certain I've never fucked a Brad.
He looks at me a bit askance, then smiles. "You moan his name when you sleep."

"Oh," I say, suddenly laughing, relieved. "You mean Brân?"
"Yeah, that's the name you're saying. Who's he?"

I moan a giant-god's name in my sleep. I guess this is weird. It's definitely queer, but no more than climbing a cliff-face in Snowdon to ask giants for help. Maybe slightly more queer than the giantess another saw straddling over me, wild, mountainous, rough. I was asleep when he saw this, in a tent amongst Alders on another land while a boar rummaged through my belongings; he was in Seattle, part-dreaming, I guess.

"He's mine, don't worry," she said to him. I wasn't there, or was—sorta. At least thirty birds had shat upon my tent and a few nearby in the morning, the only day that'd happened at that site. The Breton women camping nearby asked

if I'd seen the *sanglier* who'd come from the mountain. I hadn't, nor had I seen the giantess, either. But I had woken to snorting, muttered, 'oh—poor thing's hungry,' and had gone back to sleep.

I moan a giant-god's name in my sleep, but this is hardly all that queer. Not like the things I've seen with my eyes, the few things others have also seen along with me. The companion who asked who the massive figure was, 'leaning into me' like a muse—he saw something. The witch, though—he didn't see anything, not for a little bit, not through the searing pain that doubled him over upon the floor, naked, still erect, shouting useless curses at me. That was pretty queer.

So, too, were the druids who pulled my beard, refusing to let go 'till I pulled theirs back. Queer. Also a bit gay.

III.

Who's Brân?

Welsh king. A giant so large 'no house could hold him,' so massive he laid himself down across a river for troops to cross to the slaughter.

But to know more is where you have to go mad.

I'm trying to world in a god most don't know. Who's Brân? Might as well as who Brad is when you're drunk and naked and trying to remember all the names of the men you've fucked.

> *Flame like the searing sun and the burning fields magnified in a drop of water falling from a gnarled yew—the dragon, and the giant, and I'm impaled. Him, them, the rock under bare feet, the water raining through him, he's in the world thrust through me.*

Brân means Raven in Welsh, or Jackdaw. Jack's a giant killer, climbed a pole of the ancestors to steal back from a giant what'd been stolen. Golden eggs from a goose—there's a druid tale for you, some drunk bards spinning tales of madness because you won't believe what they actually saw.

Raven-men are all over the Welsh lore. Another one, Morfrân, 'Great Crow,' was a warrior in Arthur's court. (We'll get to that giant-killer in a bit.) Morfrân's also called Afagddu (Utter Darkness), making him in other tales the hideous child of Ceridwen for whom she brewed the potion of Awen, stolen by the boy Gwion 'by accident' to become Taliesin. And Afagddu might be a beard-flaying bear.

We know much of this from Taliesin, and Taliesin's a mad liar, awen-drunk poet slipping in and out of time and place to become everything, returning to the 'sane' with his tales. There's at least three of him, probably hundreds. He doesn't stay very well in time. Awen will do that you.

So will Brân.

IV.

I woke this morning, remembering being a mountain. I flowed down river to a city and became king of a people who weren't ready for that sort of king yet.

To learn about a god, you must go mad.

You cannot search for them as you would a job or online date. The internet's only good for all the stuff that we used a post office and a library for. But it's neither a post office nor a library—everything's short, summarized, only what someone thought you'd want to read, as opposed to what someone actually wanted to tell you.

Search for Brân and you get some stuff about the fibrous hull of a grain. In this case, it's not much worse for a Welsh giant gate-keeping god of the dead then it is for Greek gods—ask a search-engine if Apollo really exists and you've got to do some scrolling to get past moon-landing conspiracy sites.

But that's what we think we're left with, which is at least part of the reason why the world's disenchanted, the collective symptom of our shared disease, the one that's infected both this world and Others, the ones where They live, the ones where it makes sense to plant legumes to climb a world-vine to meet a giant or to hang a hundred feet above the ground to talk to one.

We place that disenchantment at different times, the moments of the turning where gods who were present—not just through poets and the mad but to everyone—suddenly withdrew. But this makes sense when we remember that all were not disenchanted at the same time; 'uncontacted' tribes in deep forests still see their spirits. Disenchantment followed dis-inheritance, displacement from land and forest into factories and mills and offices—it's hard to see a god when you're staring into machines that maul the hands, deafen the ears and dull the eyes with which we sense The Other.

That spreading plague started on the same island he's from; the laws passed to midwife in this infestation of desolation came not far from where that giant-killer dug up his head. Now, we've the internet and private property and fizzy sugar water and hand-phones but no gods and this is supposed to be better, this is supposed to be sane.

To be a poet, you must go mad, stoke 'fire in the head' searing through shining brows and steal from Ceridwen's Cauldron the elixir sought for her son Utter-Darkness

Brân had a cauldron, a gift from those he sheltered.

But Irish hospitality's a joke, at least if you're a giant. Two giants lived in Ireland and the Irish built them a house made of iron, then set it on fire to kill them. Didn't work, but the giants didn't retaliate, merely moved across the ocean, over to Wales where Brân welcomed them, let them live anywhere they wanted, unharmed. In return, they gave him their cauldron which would raise the fallen war-dead, the Cauldron of Annwn.

And later another Irish king crosses the water with a war-band, and Brân hosts them, marries off his sister Brânwen to them. To be a good host after his brother maims their horses, Brân gifts them the Cauldron of Annwn, and everything falls apart.

Risen dead, voiceless, are the gifts of that coal-black well, unherded by hounds of the underworld, freed from the rock under which they slept, pouring forth to wage battle on behalf of inhospitable peoples, fueling the machinery of war.

That—*war.*

Mistreatment of his sister sent Brân over-sea as the 'swineherds' (some readings suggest 'priests') of Ireland saw,

> *."..a forest on the ocean, where we have never seen a single tree...a great mountain beside the forest, and that was moving; and a soaring ridge on the mountain, and a lake on each side of the ridge."*

Brân the giant-king become the land, or Raven the land become the giant-king.

Brân pounds hard into the side of the head, thrusts there with the trunk of an Alder. He is a god of Alder, the warrior of Alder, the wood of shields. A mad poet knew Brân when he saw him—

> *"The high sprigs of Alder are on thy shield*
> *Bran are thou called, of the glittering branches"*

A spear pierced his ankle though maybe also his thigh (*"you dogs of Gwern, beware the pierced-thigh"*), and most see him as do I—the Fisher-King, hobbled, waiting for the unasked question in a land of desolation.

Here is a land of desolation.

Here is an unasked question.

V.

> *He leads me to the edge of a cavern, to the entrance, the gate wood and iron. "I'm moving in to where you live," he says, colors that don't exist exploding around me in those days. "I'll be there, waiting for you on the other side. Don't worry—I'm moving in." And then the druid pulls my beard, hard. And there's the woman I think I recognize but she turns and her face terrifies me. Witches, priests, druids who know something I don't yet know, and then I leave the cavern and he's there, just as he said.*

Brân punched a witch pretty hard in the stomach once. He rolled off me, naked, still erect, screaming in pain, holding his abdomen asking what the fuck I'd just done to him. I didn't do a thing, except unconsciously mutter 'thanks' to the giant-king I'd suddenly noticed, rescuing a clueless poet from a horrible event he didn't want to be part of.

Brân punches hard, his crows rip flesh, like the Ravens of The Morrigan, stripping dead flesh from crushed bone. And they're on about similar things, I guess, but also not at all, or not yet, and there's that awful war barely repaired and all those dead running lose upon the land.

War's not madness, though. Poetry is. War is machine and sanity, and the sane have trouble with giants. And some giants have trouble with us.

A king comes down from the mountains of Snowdon, from somewhere near where the dragons fought, near where Ceridwen sought the Awen for Afagddu (utter-dark) or Morfrân (great crow) from ancient Fferyllt (alchemists/metal-workers).

From amongst those giants down-river to Harlech comes a king full of giant blood—and what's giant-blood, anyway, but the water that soaks through the mountains into the soul? And there by that lake I saw the giants, there by the lake I saw shimmering dragon-fire, there by the lake I saw Brân.

Some have trouble with giants, and some giants have trouble with us, particularly [pump]Jacks and giant-killers.

There was an Arthur, or most likely was. Probably a king in the 5th and 6th century, leading Britons slowly westward as Saxons invaded, leaving finally from Cornwall to Bretagne, what the Romans called Armorica. I saw Brân too in

Armorica, by the River called Aulne (Alder), near where a giantess straddled vastly above bird-shit and a wild boar and a drunk dreaming mad poet.

The Welsh translate Satan as Arddu, generally 'great darkness.' There's a witch-cult who knows an Arddu (pronounced *Arthee*), which they name as Royal Darkness. Some of what I've heard those witches say about Arddu can also be said of Brân, but witches don't tell many tales to the uninitiated. This protects them, perhaps, but also hides the gods, and giants don't hide. But Arddu's also Arth-du, Dark Bear, and there's a giant-killer's got that name, too.

A few British Witch cults know Brân as the "lord of time," in line with Robert Graves. Mining Graves, though, like mining the dead, still leaves you with silent warriors, efficacious but unspeaking. And unraveling Arthur's a fool's game, except for poets even madder still.

Arthur slayed and subdued giants, like factories slay and subdue forests. Giants preferred the beards of men, of kings; sought them out, sheared them from their faces, slayed the resistant ones. Made clothing from them, capes and cloaks and hats, augmented their own beards. 26 lords of Britain all lost their beards and lives to one, 'till Arthur fought him and kept his. Like Jack, Arthur was a rampant giant-slayer, but there was one already dead whom he couldn't slay. From a welsh Triad:

The Three Concealments
The Head of Bran Fendigaid, ap Llyr, which was buried in the White Hill in London. and as long as the Head was there in that position, no oppression would ever come to this island
The second: the Bones of Gwerhefyr Fendigaid which were buried in the chief ports of this island
The third: the Dragons which Lludd ap Beli buried in Dinas Emrys in Eryri.

The Three Disclosures
The Bones (for the love of a woman)
The Dragons by Gwrtheyrn the Thin
The Head by Arthur because it did not seem right to him that this island should be defended by the strength of anyone other than him.

Still-speaking heads, dead speaking gods shout 'Orphic' into the spreadsheets of the sane, but here at least I understand why I found Welsh gods on a druid-mountain in France, if Dark-Bear/Utter-Dark/ Great-Crow took the King of Alder's head across a short channel with him as he fled. That Merlin's Grave, Merlin's Step, and Merlin's Well all sit in the Broceliande (*la fôret de Paimpont*), in central-west Bretagne, then makes a slight bit more sense.

VI.

> *I'm staring across a valley at a verdant hill as stormclouds gather in the gloaming evening, staring at a giant wearing a black cloak. He's as tall as the hill behind him, massive, hooded. I can't see his face or his features, only the rippling black fabric covering his form.*
>
> *There's no wind, but his cloak shakes and then starts to—to fly away, bits of fabric suddenly not fabric but wings, hundreds, thousands, perhaps millions suddenly flying towards me. They're crows—the sky is black with them, and they head past me as I stare at what's left him.*
>
> *It's only bone, white pillars where once a giant stood.*

Here we have the madness now of the poets, of how you know gods.

Brân's a giant. Brân's a raven, or a jackdaw, or a crow. Brân's the Fisher King, guardian of the bleeding lance, wounded in the thigh, waiting for the knight who will ask 'the unasked question.' The thigh is the groin, the King is barren, his lands in ruins.

In one tale, his name's Bron. In most, Percival doesn't ask, at least not 'till years of further questing to find the 'grail.' In all, the king cannot be healed 'till the question's asked.

Again that question.

I've had two visions of Brân, both inscrutable. There in the Breton mountains I saw him torn asunder by crows, crows maybe of batttle, crows likely of carrion.

And the other, the first, shakes me still, more than the gasping terror as cold fingers clung to the beard of the mountain along a cliff:

> *I stood alongside one of his bards upon a mountain, looking across to another where settled a people. Grey-black-yellow skies illumined the world below the world as their village was detroyed, flames licking their wood-and-thatch hovels.*
>
> *And time slipped around us, here in his realm. Settlers survived, built, rebuilt, now with wood and slate that did not withstand another assault. Again, brick, stone, again fire and destruction, each time the few that remained remembering, rebuilding, rebirthing upon that grand hill.*
>
> *Until the last, the greatest, towering stone walls and glass and steel, the brilliance of the Fferyllt, the height of humans here arrayed in the sunless realm.*

And then destruction, and there was no one left to rebuild.

You understand? Asked his bard who wore the features I have come to wear. There between us stood silent the unasked question as I nodded and stood before the opening gates of the dead.

Taliesin's mad ravings in The Battle of Trees has him fighting alongside Arawn, King of the Underworld as champion of those armies, and only disclosing of his identity from that Alder-shield defeats him. But Taliesin is also at Brân's side invading Ireland. He's one of the seven companions left of the armies of Wales, one of the seven who listens to the head of the giant tell tales and prophesy for decades as they sit out-of-time.

And so Brân's a lord of time, then, and Taliesin slips out with him after that battle, and later against him. But Taliesin was also the boy Gwion, accidentally stealing the three drops of Awen meant for Morfrân Giant Crow, for Afaggdu Utter-Darkness. And to obliterate finally all sanity from the soil of our soul, Taliesin leads the Dark Bear-King into Annwn to gain there the Cauldron brought by giants.

Here madness takes us if we hope to know Brân, but here sanity should flee us if we hope to survive.

It is perfectly sane to wage out your time in work, to wage war fueled by the coal-black-blood of the unspeaking dead.

It is madness to live free, to love forests, to slip out of time with gods.

From Ceridwen's Cauldron came the Awen, and those who'd drank it became mad. Speaking of the Awenyddion, a traveler in 1194, said:

> There are certain persons in Cambria, whom you will find nowhere else, called *Awenyddion*, or *people inspired*; when consulted upon any doubtful event, they roar out violently, are rendered beside themselves, and become, as it were, possessed by a spirit.

Giraldus Cambrensis, Description of Wales

I know that madness. It spun through my being while climbing a rock-face to ask giants for help to re-awaken Brân into the world; it rips through my soul in panicked moments when a god's trying to say something my small human brain is too rigid to comprehend, when suddenly you cannot stop writing until every last boiling bit of the Otherworld is wrung out of you.

The madness of the Awen-struck is the madness of the land. Taliesin shifts not only through time but through place and through beings, both in the chase of Ceridwen's rage at the theft of Awen and in the Battle of Trees, where Alder leads in the fray, where Brân is unveiled as the warrior of the Dead.

> *I have been a course, I have been an eagle.*
> *I have been a coracle in the seas:*
> *I have been compliant in the banquet.*
> *I have been a drop in a shower;*
> *I have been a sword in the grasp of the hand*
> *I have been a shield in battle.*
> *I have been a string in a harp,*
> *Disguised for nine years.*
> *in water, in foam.*

The madness of Awen is the becoming of everything, slipping through time, inhabiting place, becoming the spirits of the land and the land itself.

And it was there after the giants, after spirit in the river, after the hound at the gate, I drenched the rain soaking the mountains into giant-blood towards the sea.

The sea is everywhere, the rain soaks everyone, and giants do not sit still.

VII.

Brân is a giant, a lord of time, a god of witches, a warrior of the dead, a king in the wastes, and is the dragon of the land.

In Branwen fearch Llŷr, the Irish swineherds see the land itself rise against them, but this no surprise. We cannot blame the Irish king Matholwch for the war which brought a land against him, but rather his people. All through the tale of Brân, King Matholwch pleads for peace. He first housed the giants who brought Brân the Cauldron of the dead, 'till his people, disgusted, demanded an iron house be built to immolate them. It is the people who demand Brânwen's demeaning in the kitchen, and his people who plot to slaughter the giant in his sleep.

Here, then, the unasked question, as desolation spread outward from the city where laid buried Brâns head, disclosed so that no land-god might be relied upon for protection. From London spread the greatest plague known to us, far more virulent than the pox and Black Death, displacing peoples, disenchanting villages, destroying the forests. Mountains tumble-down upon the lakes to disclose the black-coal dead, pumpjack giant-killers siphon from the earth the blood of Annwn.

And the people cry out to the kings--what need we of gods when we have machines? What need we of a lord of time when we measure it out in hourly wages? What need we of kings when we can kill giants? What need we of madness when sanity is everywhere?

To understand a god, you must become mad. To understand madness, you must become a poet.

And here's where the maddest of them all, that Awen-thief bard slipping out of time and becoming everything, who fought alongside Brân and yet unveiled him, who stole from Ceridwen's cauldron and yet helped win it, who fled from the vengeance of a goddess and yet was birthed from her can unravel one final secret.

VIII.

Multiple gods-bothered folk have made connections between 'giants' in Celtic and the chthonic powers of the land. It's tempting to ascribe this same connection to Brân, but for a problem—Brân leaves Wales, rising up as trees, mountains and lakes across the Irish Sea to rescue his sister. Brân is not merely the land, but embodies the land and its power; the land comes with and through him.

A god shows up; people see Alder. It is the same with each Welsh god I've seen; Arianrhod is there in the shifting of light through grey-and-blue-and-violet clouds and sky reflected in water, her magic pouring from the land into the soul. In Snowdon, the lake where sought Ceridwen the ritual of Awen soaks her into your boots as you step, as giants shake rain from their shrub-beards.

Here, again, the unasked question of disenchantment. Western European societies stopped seeing the giants shaking their shrub-beards precisely at the time they began extracting the coal from their hearts to power machines to wage time into money and nature into commodity. It became 'sane' and rational to enclose land, build factories, and mete out human time according to the clocks of the Capitalist, and 'madness' to slip between those hedges, sabotage the machines, and slip out-of-time.

At the end of The Battle of Trees are three strange lines; Taliesin is not here to explain them (though on this fact I'd not wage my madness):

> *I am splendid*
> *And shall be wanton*
> *From the oppression of the metal-workers* .

A land rises up through a god through the re-enchantment of a bard against 'the oppression of the metal-workers.' The Welsh is Fferyll, perhaps the Fferyllt who held enchained in words the recipe for Awen. Taliesin's the thief there, but perhaps Ceridwen is too, manifesting from herbs, fire, and water what was locked in words, the secret of enchantment.

It is that secret we need now, awakened forests waging war, trees taking sides against each other while a mad bard dances through time and place; similar somewhat to what Lugh gains from his witches in The Second Battle of Tadgh Mor:

> *"And ye, O Be-cuile and O Dianann,"* said Lugh to his two witches, *"what power can ye wield in the battle"*
>
> *"Not hard to tell,"* said they. *"We will enchant the trees and the stones and the sods of the earth, so that they shall become a host under arms against them, and shall rout them in flight with horror and trembling."*

Brân is both the land and the god clothed in land, a giant lumbering in form of forests again against those who've stolen from the dead as in the Battle of the Trees, and the great Alder-shield who, awakened by our poetic madness, leads first amongst the warriors of the land against the oppression of the metal-workers, the giant-killing machines, and the desolation of disenchantment.

Rhyd Wildermuth is a writer, Bard, and anarchist devoted to Welsh gods. He's a monthly columnist for The Wild Hunt, writes at Paganarch.com, and is the Managing Editor for Gods&Radicals--A Site of Beautiful Resistance. He's also co-organizer of Many Gods West 2015, in Olympia, Washington. His first book, *Your Face is a Forest*, is available on Lulu.com.

Three Sisters Mountains and lava field, Oregon

© Sarah Kate Istra Winter

Made in the USA
Charleston, SC
12 August 2015